v 377.82 PAW
C3

D1236383

CATECHETICS AND PREJUDICE

CATECHETICS
AND
PREJUDICE

How Catholic Teaching Materials
View Jews, Protestants
and Racial Minorities

by
John T. Pawlikowski

MEPKIN ABBEY
1098 Mepkin Abbey Road
Moncks Corner, S.C. 29461

PAULIST PRESS
New York / Paramus / Toronto

Copyright © 1973 by
The Missionary Society
of St. Paul the Apostle
in the State of New York

Library of Congress
Catalog Card Number: 72-94109

ISBN 0-8091-1758-4

Published by Paulist Press
Editorial Office: 1865 Broadway, N.Y., N.Y. 10023
Business Office: 400 Sette Drive, Paramus, N.J. 07652

Printed and bound in the
United States of America

CONTENTS

PRENOTE

The author is indebted to a number of people who have helped carry this project forward from its conception as an independent self-study of Roman Catholic teaching materials to its culmination in this volume.

Appreciation must be expressed to Father Paul Reinert, S.J., President of St. Louis University, and Father Trafford Maher, S.J., Director of the Department of Religious Education and supervisor of the studies, for initially agreeing to undertake this project at St. Louis University at a time when Catholics were much less hospitable to public self-criticism than today.

A major debt is owed to Sisters Rose Thering, O.P., Rita Mudd, F.C.S.P., and Mary Linus Gleason, C.S.J., who pioneered the original content analyses of textbooks in, respectively, the fields of religion, social studies and literature. Their conscientious examination and critique of the materials they explored have helped pave the way for a more sensitive and accurate portrayal of non-Catholic groups in our classrooms. Moreover, appreciation is also due to their respective religious communities: the Sisters of St. Dominic, Racine, Wisconsin; the Sisters of St. Ignatius Province of the Sisters of Charity of Providence; and the

1

Sisters of St. Joseph of Wichita, Kansas, for having granted the sisters time and financial support during the period of graduate study and research.

I should like to express appreciation to Father Edward H. Flannery, Executive Secretary of the Bishops' Secretariat for Catholic-Jewish Relations, for suggesting the inclusion of concrete information on certain subjects which the studies had revealed to be inadequately treated in textbooks.

The American Jewish Committee, which conceived the project as one of a series of independent self-examinations of Protestant, Catholic and Jewish textbooks, deserves special acknowledgment for having significantly advanced impartial study in this field. In particular, I would like to express my deep gratitude to Rabbi Marc Tanenbaum, Director of Interreligious Affairs for the Committee, for his strong endorsement of the entire project and the valuable suggestions he contributed to the overall planning for publication, and to Mrs. Judith Banki, assistant director of the department, for her fine editorial work, for her valuable suggestions and research, and for her warmth and friendliness which have made collaboration with the Committee a distinct personal pleasure. I would also like to thank Fr. Terence O'Connor, O.S.M., who, as provincial of the Eastern Province of Servites, made possible my study leave at the University of Chicago during which time the substantial part of this book was completed.

Finally, a special debt of gratitude is owed to Mr. Richard C. Yalem, whose generous grant, through the Yalem Foundation, has helped to make this study possible.

FOREWORD

Prejudice seems to be linked so closely with our human condition that it is the last factor frequently to be acknowledged and confronted. It is a label that we so easily can attribute to others while absolving ourselves of any failing.

Gordon Allport, the psychologist, in *The Nature of Prejudice* describes it as an avertive or hostile attitude. Apart from its latent form, oftentimes resulting from lack of information, limited field of experience and a tendency to generalize or caricature, prejudice does manifest affective qualities in its *All in the Family* form— hostility, contempt, bias and collectivizing.

Although the starting point for this thought-provoking book may appear dated (namely, three studies of the attitudes toward racial, ethnic and religious groups in the fields of literature, social studies and religious education, completed at St. Louis University a decade ago, under the sponsorship of the American Jewish Committee), one legitimately might wonder if the findings have been superseded substantially and widely.

Despite a decade of significant ecumenical and interreligious advances and declarations, broad-scale attitudinal bias may still remain. Touching upon social studies and literature the scope of this book falls within the wider understanding of catechesis. Social relations and interactions form the basis for the expression of our religious values and beliefs. It is one thing to affirm brotherhood and dignity; it is another to live it out and observe how it has been concretely manifested in the history of men's social relations.

Philip Phenix of Columbia Teachers College has urged that teachers should assist their students in developing an ability of "disciplined intersubjectivity." The student is enabled to transcend his own limited world and enter imaginatively and sympathetically into the other person's world with his values, outlooks and background. This acquires a new urgency in our present day when the study of world religions and religious themes in public school literature and social studies courses (frequently described as the "objective study of religion") is becoming commonplace.

There are conflicting forces at work in these days. We note an increasing demand for racial, ethnic and religious identity at odds with the mystic quest for assimilation and identification with the predominant values and culture of the majority group in society. It is evident how both trends can lead to subtle and even not so subtle forms of bias and prejudice.

For the religion teacher and interested adult *Catechetics and Prejudice* offers a contemporary re-examination of some of the sources of religious bias especially against the chosen people. The role of the biblical-age Pharisees as a progressive force of renewal, the objective understanding of the passion and death of Jesus, new attitudes toward the two major covenants, the relationship of St. Paul to Judaism and a critical understanding of biblical texts are discussed with precision and scope.

Fr. Edward Flannery proposes a distinction between anti-Semitism with its affective elements of hostility and contempt and anti-Judaism which connotes a more intellectual, discriminating opposition. In our efforts to put our students in contact with the valuable findings of sound biblical exegesis, the theological intent of the New Testament authors and the church setting and situation (such as the confrontation between church and synagogue) must be weighed and considered.

What is needed is a re-Judaizing of our religious perspectives and thoughtful reassessing of our own attitudes, presumptions and bias. This important book should help all sensitive and concerned teachers and leaders to appreciate the on-going contribution of our Jewish brothers, and especially, as Fr. Pawlikowski notes, their emphasis on the importance of history, man's responsibility for creation, the quest for salvation in community and the encouraging truth that man is not basically evil.

Rev. William J. Tobin
Assistant Director
National Center of Religious Education—CCD
Washington, D.C.

CHAPTER 1

INTRODUCING THE STUDIES

A landmark in ecumenical education has been achieved over the past few decades through scientific studies of religious instructional materials under the sponsorship of the American Jewish Committee. While its primary goal has been the protection of the civil and religious rights of Jews, the Committee has pioneered a number of studies aimed at understanding the dynamics of all forms of prejudice. Beginning in the 1930's and culminating in the 50's and 60's, the Committee initiated textbook studies by Protestants, Catholics and Jews of their own teaching materials. Basic to these projects was the notion of *self-study*. Criticism of the materials was to come from within the tradition that produced them.

The choice of religious instructional materials for such research was not haphazard. Among Jewish and Christian scholars alike, the conviction was widespread and deeply implanted that a certain tradition of Christian teaching, uncritically handed down for generations, was a prime source of anti-Semitism. Edward Flannery traces the roots of this tradition as far back as the third century:

More ominous was the emergence of a teaching not yet fully

formulated but clearly enunciated in St. Hippolytus and Origen: that Jews are a people punished for their deicide who can never escape their misfortunes, which are willed of God. This thesis formed the first seeds of an attitude that would dominate Christian thinking in the fourth century and greatly contribute thereafter to the course of anti-Semitism.[1]

Gregory Baum has also acknowledged the problem:

It is true that Christian literature . . . in later centuries has elaborated the teachings of the Gospel to create a weapon for the struggle against Judaism. Christian authors have covered the mystery of Israel with theological embroidery which has contributed to the contempt and the debasement of the Jewish people, and these theories have become so much entangled with the Church's teaching that they have formed the mentality of generations, of whole centuries, even to our own day.[2]

The systematic denigration of Jews and Judaism in Christian teaching and preaching, accompanied for much of Western history by harsh and restrictive legislation against Jews—in fact, often serving as the pretext for anti-Semitism—is an unfortunate legacy from earlier periods of conflict. In similar vein, bitter conflicts between Catholics and Protestants are also part of the common Christian inheritance. The question remained whether religious textbooks were promoting prejudice toward other groups— religious, racial or ethnic.

The studies were placed in the hands of educational specialists at Yale University (Protestant), St. Louis University (Catholic), and Dropsie College (Jewish).

The Protestant section of the project was directed by the Rev. Dr. Bernhard E. Olson at Yale University. He examined some 120,000 religious school lesson plans and texts of four major Protestant publishers, representing the major trends in the Protestant community, from conservative to liberal. The results of his seven-year study were published in 1963 under the title *Faith and Prejudice*.[3] Dr. Olson's thorough analysis of the intergroup content in Protestant teaching prompted President John C. Bennett of Union Theological Seminary to assert that "consciously or unconsciously, the seeds of prejudice are in religious teachings."[4]

Theologian Reinhold Niebuhr, upon examinating the findings, remarked that religious sources of anti-Semitism may be more powerful than racial sources.

The Jewish textbook study was supervised by Dr. Bernard D. Weinryb at Dropsie College in Philadelphia. He examined over 200 pieces of classroom material in English, Hebrew and Yiddish, including books, plays and periodicals, drawn from 46 organizations and individual Jewish publishers. He found that the Jewish instructional materials were generally non-directional (neither positive nor negative) in their approach to other religious groups, with the historical approach most prominent. Criticism was usually limited to specific representatives of religious outgroups rather than to the group as a whole, with the exception of some materials based on folk legends coming from East European Jewry. It should be noted that only 14.4 percent of the Jewish materials concerned themselves with outside religious groups, in contrast to 51.4 percent of the Catholic materials and 66.5 to 87.9 percent of the Protestant materials examined in the AJC-sponsored studies. Dr. Weinryb concludes that on the whole the Jewish school curriculum is more introverted than its Catholic or Protestant counterparts.[5]

The Catholic portion of the textbook self-studies, to which this book is devoted, was placed under the direction of Father Trafford P. Maher, S.J., of the sociology department at St. Louis University. He divided the Catholic study into three areas: literature, social studies and religion. Each area eventually became subject matter for a doctoral dissertation by a member of the department. An analysis of Catholic high school texts in history, geography, civics and social studies was produced by Sister M. Rita Mudd, F.S.C.P.,[6] while Sister M. Linus Gleason, C.S.J.,[7] examined high school literature materials. The study of religious textbooks was undertaken by Sister Rose Thering, O.P.[8]

It is interesting to note that Sister Thering's study was the last in the Catholic series. This was deliberate. The project directors were concerned at the time that criticism of religious texts, which in Sister Thering's words had achieved a kind of "sanctity by association," might outrage many Catholics. Hence the decision to concentrate first on literature and social studies. Here we have a reflection of the mind-set of the pre-Vatican II Church as well as an indication of how far we have advanced today, partly through the courageous work of such people as Sisters Mudd, Gleason and Thering.

The research explored attitudes toward racial and ethnic as well as religious groups. Each of the researchers tried to express in statistical form the degree of positive or negative attitudes towards non-white ethnic groups and non-Catholic religious communities by examining a number of widely used textbook series. While home, school, and peer groups may be more influential in forming attitudes, textbooks are one possible source of prejudicial misconceptions of other groups. As Sister Thering puts it, "They [textbooks] affect the formation of habits of kindliness, understanding and love toward other groups—or the opposite of these habits."[9] The disturbing question thus arises: Do Catholic textbooks reflect actual Christian teachings?

The potential dangers inherent in textbook misrepresentations have been recognized for some time. This past century has witnessed a host of textbook analyses dealing with such topics as slavery, patriotism, Anglo-American relations, racial attitudes, and so on. In the last decade school board battles over the adoption of texts have become more and more frequent. One of UNESCO's aims has been the examination of textbooks from member nations in the hope of eradicating chauvinism and factual errors.

The possible "halo" effect of religious texts has been variously noted. Existing negative attitudes, which are unrelated to the substance of faith, or even at variance with it, may acquire religious sanction in a student's mind. Should they become an integral part of his world picture during this crucial stage of intellectual and emotional development, they are very difficult to change at a later stage. Comments about long-dead Jews and Protestants may influence attitudes toward twentieth-century Jewish and Protestant neighbors.

The French writer, Paul Démann, who was inspired by the pioneering work of the great French historian Jules Isaac in the area of religious teaching and prejudice, studied references to Jews in Catholic texts in France in the early fifties. He summed up the danger of textbook distortion in this way:

10

The Jews whom they [the students] learn about in the catechism, in sermons, in reading, will be, for many Christians, the first ones and sometimes the only ones they will ever meet. The impression which they receive will determine, for the most part, the opinions and dispositions of heart with which they will approach the Jews who will cross their path. . . . This will be either a feeling of respect and sympathy towards the Chosen People of God, descendants of the saints of the Old Testament, our ancestors in faith . . . of Jesus, Mary, and the first disciples; or it will be a feeling of aversion and scorn, of secret hostility toward a perfidious, condemned, fallen and cursed people, killers of God.[10]

Often it is not the presentation of doctrine itself as much as gratuitous bias that brings about negative reactions from the student. Culture-bound non-essentials too easily become integrated with the substance of religious belief and conduct. Such distortions can appear and reappear with the stubborn tenacity of crabgrass. Such bias not only proves harmful to intergroup relations but eventually corrodes genuine religious values within the group itself.

Those familiar with recent educational changes in the United States are well aware that textbooks no longer are as central to the educational process as in previous decades. The high school level in particular has seen a trend of increased reliance on primary sources. Yet textbooks are still very much an important part of the educational picture. This is especially true on the primary level. And though textbooks are to serve as a tool for the teacher and not his master, print gives a measure of force and authority to the spoken word, as Sister Thering notes in her study.[11] While a teacher should look upon a textbook as no more than a springboard to creative instruction in the classroom, it still remains a basic instrument for many teachers and an important tool in the hands of the student. All this is to say that the textbook continues to be an important force in attitudinal formation toward other religious and ethnic groups.

Some may object that the textual materials which formed the basis of the three Catholic analyses are no longer in general use and hence the findings derived from them are of little current value. This objection requires a forthright answer. Certainly, significant changes have occurred in recent textbook series, primarily as a result of Vatican II and the influence of these studies. A joint Catholic-Jewish study team in the archdiocese of Atlanta, for example, discovered considerable improvement in post-Vatican II textbooks in comparison to pre-conciliar materials. But even in these improved materials some anti-Jewish passages were found to remain.[12]

Many reputable Catholic publishers now ask members of the Protestant and Jewish communities to read through manuscripts prior to publication. Rabbi Edward Zerin served in this capacity for some five years and he recorded his experiences in *CCAR Journal*.[13] He found much unevenness among Catholic ecumenical endeavors, some being positive, creative efforts which in his opinion should be welcomed and "both complimented and complemented." He cites as an example the following statement which now forms part of a chapter on pluralism in the *To Live Is Christ* (Vol. I) series published by Henry Regnery Co.:

But you must realize that being Catholic does not necessarily make you better than anyone else. . . . There are many Protestants, Jewish persons and non-believers who are more faithful to their consciences than some Catholics are to theirs. . . . We must beware of a "Catholic superiority complex," not only as private individuals, but as a group. . . . While we believe our *doctrines* are true, we must admit that our *customs* may not always be the best way to express our doctrines. . . . (pp. 97-98). So we live today in what is called a *pluralistic* society—that is, one which is based on many ("plural") beliefs, rather than just one way of thinking. . . . (p. 95).

Nonetheless other texts have been recently prepared (but not published) by Catholic authors which, according to Rabbi Zerin, "still exhibit the hand of the medieval artisan." He offers the following example:

We differ in this: We Catholics believe that "a partial blindness only has befallen Israel" (Rom. 11:25). We believe that, because most Jews do not accept Jesus as the Messiah, we who are wild olive branches have been grafted into the cultivated tree of God's choice. We believe that, because they do not believe in Jesus as the Messiah, the Jewish people are temporarily cut off from the tree to which they belong by a right prior to ours.

Nor are such problems limited to the United States. *The New York Times* reported that a pejorative image of Jews and Judaism was still to be found in Roman Catholic religious textbooks used in the world's French-speaking areas. The study was conducted by a team of scholars at Louvain University's (Belgium) Center for Socio-Religious Research and the Center for Catechetical Studies in cooperation with the American Jewish Committee's Leonard M. Sperry Center for Intergroup Cooperation. The director of the study, sociologist Francois Houtart, said that the texts examined, whose potential readership was 60 million people in France, Belgium, Canada and Switzerland, still depicted the Jews of Jesus' time as materialists who were collectively to blame for his crucifixion. Some textbooks examined in this study presented the Jewish biblical notion of the Messiah as a man who would enhance the material prosperity of the Jews. The study concluded:

The heart of the problem of the presentation of Jews in catechetical teaching is that Jews still remain as typical examples of non-believers of bad faith. They are examples not to be followed, serving as a foil contrasting with a Christian attitude.[14]

Similarly, a study of Italian and Spanish religion textbooks revealed substantial hostility to Judaism and other non-Roman Catholic faiths three years after the Vatican Council *Declaration on the Relationship of the Church to non-Christian Religions.* The study, as reported in *The New York Times,*[15] was carried out by four scholars, assisted by sixteen experts, under the auspices of the Leonard M. Sperry Center for Intergroup Cooperation at the Free International University of Social Studies Pro Deo, an institution recognized by the Holy See. "We are struck," concluded the authors, "by the large amount of hostility, not only against Jews, but against other groups as well in both the Italian and Spanish samples." Offered in evidence was one example from an

Italian textbook:

From that time [the crucifixion] the curse of God has fallen on this people [the Jews], which for more than nineteen centuries has been scattered over the earth, the object of hatred and mistrust, without country, without altar, without priest.

Thus, despite improvements in recent textbooks, the problem of prejudice and distortion in Catholic teaching materials remains very much with us.

The findings of the historic St. Louis studies have additional contemporary value. The studies point not only to specific examples of prejudiced writing—many of which have been superseded —but to the problem *areas:* those themes, instances of historical or religious conflict, around which negative judgments of other groups tend to concentrate. They also indicate the lacunae—the places where distortion is present not by intent, but by failure to provide constructive or corrective information. Knowledge of the studies can thus be invaluable in sensitizing Catholic teachers both to aspects of the curriculum with a hidden but potent intergroup impact, and to areas where they can round out inadequate presentations. Such sensitizing is particularly important as teachers are offered increasingly more creative freedom in selecting supplementary classroom materials.

This freedom, along with increased reliance on primary sources, is a welcome development, but it does impose additional responsibilities on the individual teacher to choose wisely.

Indeed, the entire question of teachers' attitudes comes into focus at this point. It must be acknowledged that many Catholic teachers, educationally speaking, are a result of the same mindset that produced the earlier textbooks. Moreover, relatively few have been exposed to the process of analysis and re-evaluation which has resulted in so much textbook revision. With the best will in the world, many teachers do not fully understand or appreciate the changes that have taken place or the need for additional revision in a number of areas. Rather than rehearse the gaps and weaknesses revealed by the St. Louis studies, the author has included a number of positive recommendations and, in some cases, specific information which he hopes will be helpful.

The recommendations offered to round out inadequate presentations of racial and ethnic groups are general in tone. More specific information is provided in the area of teaching about Jews and Judaism. There are several reasons for this. First, many Christians are unaware of the long history of persecution of Jews so frequently justified in the past by Christian pretexts. Another reason is the high visibility of Jewish references in Catholic religion materials. A third is the hesitancy and uncertainty among teachers about the full implications of the new attitude toward the Jewish people. An analysis of the questionnaire given to Catholic teachers in an institute on Judaism, directed by Sister Rose Thering and myself in Chicago, indicates that the teachings were not able to fully harmonize the negative portrayal of Judaism in the New Testament with the new post-Vatican II approach.[16]

This confusion is a reflection of profound problems, many of which have not yet been resolved. Nevertheless, the author believes that there is value in spelling out the remaining problems and indicating where current Christian thought is moving, even if no final answers exist as yet.

FOOTNOTES

1. Edward H. Flannery, *The Anguish of the Jews,* New York: Macmillan, 1965, p. 43.
2. Gregory Baum, *The Jews and the Gospel,* New York: Newman Press, 1961, p. 5.
3. New Haven: Yale University Press.
4. Cf. James W. Arnold, "Religious Textbooks . . . Primers in Bigotry," New York: The American Jewish Committee, p. 2.
5. Cf. Bernard D. Weinryb and Daniel Garnick, "Summary of Findings, The Dropsie College Study of Jewish Textbooks: 'Jewish School Textbooks and Intergroup Relations,' " New York: The American Jewish Committee.
6. *Intergroup Relations in Social Studies Curriculum.* Unpublished doctoral dissertation, St. Louis University, 1961.
7. *Intergroup Relations as Revealed by Content Analysis of Literature Textbooks Used in Catholic Secondary Schools.* Unpublished doctoral dissertation, St. Louis University, 1958.
8. *Potential in Religious Textbooks for Developing a Realistic Self Concept.* Unpublished doctoral dissertation, St. Louis University, 1961.

15

9. Cf. James W. Arnold, *op. cit.*, p. 3.
10. *Ibid.*
11. Cf. Sister Rose Thering, *op. cit.*, p. 11.
12. Cf. Sister Mary Alice Muir, S.N.D. de N., "Catholic-Jewish Team Review Textbooks," *The Christian Century,* January 15, 1969, p. 99.
13. Cf. *CCAR Journal,* June 1969, p. 80.
14. Eric Pace, "Catholic Panel Finds Pejorative Image of Judaism in French Religious Texts," *The New York Times,* October 12, 1969, p. 45.
15. Robert Doty, "Anti-Semitic References Found in Italian and Spanish Texts Three Years after Ban by Vatican Council," *The New York Times,* June 29, 1969.
16. "Summary and Interpretation of Questionnaires Given to Catholic Teachers on Judaism," Chicago: Catholic Adult Education Center, 1968.

CHAPTER 2

GENERAL FINDINGS

Before proceeding to an analysis of what the St. Louis textbook studies reveal about Catholic attitudes towards specific ethnic, racial and religious outgroups, some general observations about the overall findings will be useful.* The studies unveiled a striking discrepancy in the amount of intergroup content found in the religion materials when compared to the social studies and literature texts. Over half of the religion units dealt with outside religious, racial or ethnic groups. But in the literature materials the picture changed dramatically. With a few exceptions black and Oriental characters are almost non-existent. One literature set (four books) had only fifteen characters identifiable as black and none of them occupied a major role in the narrative. The American Indian and non-Christian groups were represented only rarely in the literature materials.

The results of the literature study pose a serious dilemma for the teacher interested in intergroup relations. Teachers obviously must apply good literary standards as their primary criterion in the selection of classroom texts. No one would advocate choosing inferior literature simply because it had a high intergroup orienta-

*Research procedures are described in the Appendix.

17

tion. Nonetheless, given the social tensions of our day and realizing the powerful effect literature can have on the attitudes of students, the intergroup aspect cannot be totally ignored in the selection of materials. Special efforts must be made to locate materials that have merit as literature as well as expose the student in a positive way to characters clearly identifiable as non-white and non-Catholic. At the primary and secondary levels literature courses must be viewed within the broader context of the total curriculum whose aim must be the socialization of the student. Hence the goal of pre-college literature classes is somewhat different from the goal of a literature course on the college level. The primary and secondary student is usually more confined in his contacts. As a result, literary characters may be the closest he will come to meeting in a positive way members of minority ethnic, religious and racial groups. While no precise guidelines can be laid down, it is imperative that the teacher of literature in primary and secondary schools be sensitive to the problems of intergroup relations and the special contribution literature can make in presenting "living" minority characters.

The social studies texts showed the least intergroup content. Only slightly more than 5 percent of the materials contained intergroup references, and over 80 percent of the intergroup references that were isolated eventually fell into the neutral or nondirectional category. In other words, of the 28,629 pages subject to analysis, only 304 (cumulative) pages presented the student with positive attitudes toward other groups.

The results of the social studies survey are especially alarming. While it is somewhat understandable that literature materials might lack a high degree of intergroup content, social studies texts should have better intergroup relations as a central goal. The findings would seem to offer a serious indictment against the social studies texts used in Catholic instruction in the recent past. No doubt the absence of any real confrontation with the problem of social relations in American life reflects the general malaise on this problem that characterized American thinking until the last few years. The tensions of today had not yet surfaced. But the sufferings of black men, Jews, Indians, and Orientals were there and it is unfortunate that Catholic students of a generation ago were not being prepared to cope with the challenges presented by American social discrimination. Perhaps if they had, some of the problems facing us today would not have become so intense. When minority groups charge the Church with really failing to come to grips with the social and economic inequalities in American society, the seeming indifference of the social studies materials to these inequalities certainly tends to confirm their judgment. The social studies texts examined in the St. Louis project clearly did not prepare their students to become leaders in the struggle against injustice in our country.

The visibility of the various religious and ethnic groups differs according to the nature of the materials. As might be expected, the religion textbooks are much more preoccupied with non-Catholic religious groups than with outside racial or ethnic groups. Of the combined total of intergroup references, 69 percent had to do with other religious groups, 16 percent fell into the "general" category (i.e., discussions of the brotherhood of man, broad references to "all men," etc.), and 15 percent referred to specific racial, ethnic and international groups.

Within the religion materials Jews were by far the most conspicuous group. In many of the texts, references to Jews constituted more than half of all the references to non-Catholic groups, reaching a high of 84.1 percent in one series of materials. The high visibility of Jews and Judaism in Catholic religion materials is understandable in view of the Jewish origins of Christianity. It is obvious that Christianity cannot be presented theologically or historically without some reference to Abraham, the prophets, the history of Israel, the Jewishness of Jesus and his disciples, and the conflict between the early Church and synagogue. The textbook prominence of a group which, on the one hand, played so central a role in the birth of the Church and, on the other hand, continues to exist as a distinct religio-ethnic community in the contemporary world, creates special problems for intergroup understanding. Textbook writers may not always be aware that comments made about "the Jews" in a first-century setting may influence feelings and attitudes toward twentieth-century neighbors.

Protestants were the second most visible group in the religion materials. They were mentioned with greater consistency than either Eastern Christians or non-Christians.

It is important to contrast the visibility of Jews and Judaism in the religion materials with their less than central position in the social studies texts (where Protestants and non-Christians are more visible) and above all in the literature materials where they are virtually non-existent. When one realizes that the vast majority of the references in the religion materials focus on the biblical period, it becomes evident that Catholic students have been deprived of meaningful exposure to post-biblical Judaism in their studies. This cannot but foster an attitude which sees Judaism as anachronistic. Since many Catholic students grow up in large metropolitan areas which contain a substantial Jewish population, this lack of exposure to contemporary Judaism constitutes a serious gap in their socialization process.

Some general conclusions from the St. Louis examination of religion textbooks may be summarized as follows. First of all, it is clear that when the textbooks under analysis focused on such broad concepts as the fatherhood of God and the brotherhood of men, or referred to outgroups in general terms, their comments were overwhelmingly positive. The general intergroup references, however, accounted for only 16 percent of the total intergroup content.

The religion materials showed a similar positive disposition toward racial and ethnic groups, especially black Americans. Treatment of racial-ethnic groups was also extremely positive. Statements regarding racial and ethnic groups, however, made up only 15 percent of the scored references. When we come to non-Catholic religious groups, where the great bulk (69 percent) of the intergroup content was located, the scores drop sharply.

The sharp contrasts between the general and specific religious group scores indicate a significant difference in the way racial and ethnic groups were portrayed in the materials and the picture drawn of religious outgroups. The problems of identifying in a positive manner with other religions appear to be more difficult and more complex than those connected with inter-racial and inter-ethnic relationships. This situation may be partly due to the avoidance of the real conflicts in racial and ethnic relations in this country by the religion texts. But the St. Louis studies clearly show how difficult it is to identify with one's own religious group and retain at the same time an appreciation of the particular beliefs of other religious communities. This is especially true of the relationship of Judaism and Christianity, Judaism-Christianity and Islam, and Catholicism and Protestantism. For in the chronological development of these religions each has claimed to be the true successor of its parent(s), and the separations have been accompanied by intense historical conflict, frequently by warfare and bloodshed. There is an understandable tendency to define one's own faith in contradistinction to the claims of competing faiths, and to emphasize the suffering and martyrdom endured by one's own co-religionists at the hands of others. In the absence of corrective or balancing information, such an approach would be roughly the equivalent of American history textbooks mentioning, say, England, only in the context of its enmity to the United States and the wars fought between the two nations. Students would get at best a fragmentary picture of English history from such a presentation, and no sense of a separate ongoing English tradition, of which conflict with the United States may be only a small part.

Our analogy suggests that our concept of other groups should not be formed predominantly by citing situations of conflict with them. Still, the conflicts are historical realities and every group must be true to its own history in educating its students. The St. Louis studies do not provide easy answers to this difficult question, but they do bring us face to face with the depth of the problems involved in a truly ecumenical outlook, and they clearly reaffirm the continued centrality of specific religious traditions in modern man's self-identification, if for no other reason than the fact that the religion materials were the last to be examined. As previously noted, this decision was deliberately taken because of a fear that criticism of religion materials might engender an outcry in the Catholic community. Religious instructional materials were assumed to have a "sacred" aspect that the literature and social

21

studies units did not, an indication of how closely religious teachings are tied to the basic life stance of an individual.

The St. Louis findings also testify that vague general appeals to the brotherhood of all men are no substitute for an in-depth study of the tensions that have existed between the major religious traditions throughout history. In fact, platitudes about brotherhood may do nothing more than cover up tension areas in a superficial way, deluding us into thinking we have real agreement when we do not. And then we open ourselves to shock and disillusionment when serious differences arise on substantive issues.

The way in which statements of good will about mankind or other groups in general may break down when specific cases of conflict with specific non-Catholic faith groups come into the open is exemplified in the St. Louis study of religion textbooks. Sister Thering provided 173 representative quotations from the examined materials to illustrate the range of statements about outside groups. While these do not cover the total group content of the textbooks, they do provide an adequate sampling.

Of the 173 samples, 61 came under the "general" classification, statements such as "All men are created equal" or "Christ makes charity the special sign of his followers: 'By this shall all men know you are my disciples, if you have love for one another.' " These 61 references amassed a total of 138 positive scores, 5 neutral and no negative scores. But when the results for specific non-Catholic religious groups were analyzed, the statistical picture changed radically. Sixty-two of the 173 representative examples referred to Jews and Judaism. Their scores were 50 negative, 38 positive and 27 neutral. Thirty of the examples referred to Protestants, with an accumulated total of 41 negative scores, 8 neutral and 5 positive scores.

The following examples bring out well the gap between general statements of brotherhood and the treatments of particular groups.

General Example

Every person in the world is your neighbor whether he is black, brown, yellow or white; whether he lives in the western or eastern half of the world; whether he can talk English or not; whether he is a Christian, Jew, Protestant, or pagan; whether he is young or old, a gentleman or a fool, a Republican or a Democrat; whether he knows the latest song hits, the latest baseball scores and the latest slang. That gives you about 1,900,000,000 neighbors.

Specific Examples

Protestantism granted concessions in an attempt to attract all who lacked courage to live up to the high standards proposed by Christ and the Church. Protestantism today is rapidly deteriorating, while the unchanging spiritual church grows ever stronger with the years.

Why did the Jews commit the great sin of putting God himself to death? It was because our Lord told them the truth, because he preached a divine doctrine that displeased them, and because he told them to give up their wicked ways.

In the social studies materials, the discrepancy between affirmations of brotherhood and negative attitudes toward specific outgroups is far less intense. (But there are far fewer references to specific outgroups than in the religion textbooks.) The weakness of the social studies materials is their silence on intergroup problems. Still, there is some significance in the lack of a sudden drop in positive scores as one moves from general to specific references in the social studies materials. There are even positive attempts to counteract specific distortions of outgroups which the authors feel to be commonplace among Catholics or white Americans.

The social studies materials generally maintain that various cultures have left a beneficial impact on American life, that our nation has been built by many races, colors and creeds. This is expressed by the writers in various ways. Some speak of our "pluralistic culture," while others rely on the term "American mosaic." The "melting pot" concept is found in only one or two publications, in quotation marks. And in each case the author explains that "unity with diversity" would be a better way to express the Americanization of our various peoples. Diversity within unity is stressed as advantageous. Diversity contributes richness and unity gives strength.

23

In their appeal for brotherhood, the social studies textbooks rely on both the principles of American democracy and the Catholic ideal of the equality of all men. The latter is explained again and again in the materials as rooted in man's creation in the image of God and in his eternal destiny to live with God. Stress is laid on nature's gift of liberty to each man whereby he possesses a power over his actions and personal rights that can neither be given nor taken away by any human agency.

The following quotations are a good sample of both the positive and negative presentation of outgroups that appear in the social studies texts.

Positive Examples

Since the English, with their customs and institutions, formed the majority in the colonies, English culture forms the basis of our own. But our culture is *not* English. That basis has been so changed in the course of time by close contact with the cultures of all nations that a definitely American culture is emerging. *Each* immigrant culture adds color and beauty of its own and is shaped by contact with other cultures to fit into the whole design. All of us working in our own way, according to the best dictates of our hearts and consciences, are helping to build America. No two of us work exactly alike; each one colors his contribution by the unique and individual force of his own nationality and personality. All are used; all are useful. Each one of us is a part of a giant system, marvelous and intricate, delicate yet majestic. As we work, we should be aware of a giant purpose, of the limitless possibilities of our work.

Typical of mistaken judgment is the statement that by heredity Negroes are mentally inferior to whites, and therefore it is a mistake to try to provide higher education for them.

To denounce anti-Semitism is not enough to defeat it. The best way to treat this question is to examine and expose some of the foundations on which it rests. The statement is made that the Jews control American industry. The magazine *Fortune,* in an impartial survey made some years ago, showed that this is not true. Jews do not dominate banking, the automobile, rubber, oil, coal, or transportation industries. They have, however, a dominant place in the textile field. Their ownership of newspapers and magazines is small in proportion to the total number of publications but their influence is great. Only in radio, the theater, and the moving picture industry can the Jews be said to have the controlling interest. In these fields the public makes the ultimate decision as to what is offered. . . . Have the Jews overcrowded the professions? Fifty percent of the lawyers and one-third of the physicians in New York are Jewish. But the professions are open to all who are willing to undergo the extensive and rigorous preparation required. Does the Jew advance in business . . . ? He should not be denied the fruits of his ambition and perseverance.

The attitude of national superiority that accompanied our overseas adventures was at the time [of our imperialism and power politics] a kind of American arrogance that sometimes dulled our feelings for the rights of others.

The exploitation of the immigrants and the conditions under which they lived was a discredit to the American people.

Negative Examples

The Blackfoot Indians of Montana never stopped looking for revenge.

Although the Jewish people rejected the redeemer when he came into their midst, the divine plan of God was definitely accomplished.

After the rejection of Christ and his crucifixion by the Jews, their Holy City was destroyed in 70 A.D.

The Protestant revolt led to bitter intolerance and war; it led to an intensification of nationalism, the capitalistic spirit, absolutism, and secularization.

Christ told the Jews they rejected him, not because of their love for the old religion, but because of their evil ways.

Islam has been a source of dissension among the peoples of the world.

Some reflections on the difference between the findings regarding social studies textbooks and religion textbooks may be in order here. Statistically, the social studies materials show a high positive score when dealing both with the theme of brotherhood in general and with specific outgroups in particular. The religion materials score high on brotherhood in the abstract, but the scores drop sharply when specific non-Catholic religious groups are discussed. This might lead the unwary to conclude that the American spirit of equality invoked in the social studies textbooks is a more pervasive motivating force for positive outgroup portraiture than the Christian theory of the brotherhood of all men. I believe such a judgment would bypass one of the great problems facing Catholic education today. That problem is finding the real path from the Christian ideal of brotherhood to its implementation in the concrete reality of society. Insofar as the findings of the social studies analysis indicate we have made the transition successfully, I suggest they are misleading. The spirit of equality and brotherhood presented in the social studies materials seems more and more in our time to appear superficial and perhaps deceptive. The principle frequently employed in the St. Louis studies for evaluating "positive" references is questionable in that it appears to value the assimilation of outgroups into the dominant cultural and life-style patterns of the American white Christian majority. Thus, in many of the statements scored as "positive," students are told to esteem non-whites and non-Christians because "they are really like us white Christians." This conception, implying universal adoption of a cultural norm set by the patterns of a majority, seems shallow today, when blacks, Indians, Mexican Americans, Puerto Ricans, Jews and Orientals have begun to demand that they be respected for their differences from white Christian Americans as well as for their similarities.

I do not intend to downplay the valuable contribution that the American spirit of toleration has made in many areas, nor to imply that the researchers of the St. Louis studies were guilty of prejudice in their determination of "positive" statements. It is simply that we have come a long way in the few short years since the St. Louis studies were made. We can no longer assume that people are to be valued because "they are really like us."

This is certainly not to say that all of the positively scored statements in the St. Louis studies reflected a patronizing tone. The passage quoted above regarding the *Fortune* investigation of the place of the Jew in American economic life, for example, exhibited a real sensitivity for the depth of the prejudice and discrimination non-whites and non-Christians have experienced in our nation. But many of the treatments seem superficial in today's perspective.

In this sense, paradoxically, negative passages found in the religion texts may be a more honest reflection of reality than many of the positive references in the social studies units.

We are engaged in a new struggle to understand the relationship between particularity—ethnic and religious—and universality in our pluralistic society. The problem is not unique to our shores; the American historian John Hope Franklin has shown that every major country is now facing a challenge from a non-integrated minority group. But the situation in the United States is more complex than elsewhere because our national self-image and our integrity throughout the world depend to a large extent on how we fulfill our pluralistic claims. If we fail to understand the new thrust for genuine identity among America's minority groups, or attempt to resolve tensions by confinement or repression (as we did to Americans of Japanese descent during World War II), our nation may lose its soul completely. Can the American mosaic become a reality and not merely a slogan? Can our minorities become part of the American mainstream without sacrificing their ethnicity in the process? Jews represent a good example of the facade of much of the present American mosaic. Their seeming assimilation has been only peripheral. They stand outside the real centers of power in this country, where most decisions affecting their lives are made. American culture does little to express distinctive Jewish values despite its claim to be "Judaeo-Christian." Thus, many Jews are fearful of playing the role of scapegoat as internal or international tensions and conflicts escalate.

Obviously, the challenge of forging an authentic pluralism does not rest only with the Catholic educational system. It is a challenge for society as a whole. But to the extent to which our

27

teaching materials and our teachers themselves influence students' attitudes, we have an important role to play.

In the following chapters we will examine specific findings for each of the major ethnic and religious groups encountered in the St. Louis studies. Special emphasis will be placed on the Jewish group because of its high visibility in the religion materials and because its portrait in Christian teaching points to some specific problems.

CHAPTER 3

THE PORTRAITS OF RACIAL
AND ETHNIC GROUPS

The St. Louis studies revealed an overwhelmingly positive orientation to racial and ethnic groups. In the religion materials, the scores for racial-ethnic groups were exceeded only by those for general statements on brotherhood, and surpassed by far those for the religious group category. The social studies materials showed scores for the racial-ethnic category that were slightly lower than those recorded for the religion materials but still very much positive in outlook. Once again, in the social studies materials, the scores for racial-ethnic groups were considerably better than the scores recorded for religious group references.

The literature materials exposed a similar situation. In all the literature units examined by the researcher, the Caucasoid race predominated in numbers and in educational status. Yet the treatment accorded minority groups with regard to roles and positive character traits showed that in some ways the minority groups were more favorably presented than the Caucasoids. These literature results, however, raise the question of the dangers of the "halo treatment" of minorities. In one of the literary sets analyzed in the study, black characters rated higher than Caucasoids in prudence, honesty, respectability and desirability. Mongoloids

29

MEPKIN ABBEY
1098 Mepkin Abbey Road
Moncks Corner, S.C. 29461

scored slightly higher than Caucasoids in prudence and honesty but fell somewhat behind them in the areas of respectability and desirability. Despite these apparently positive statistics, there remains an unrealistic, fairy-tale, composite character about the minority groups, especially in the case of black people. Not one black character was depicted as imprudent. The minority characters, particularly the blacks, seem to lack any backbone, which may indicate an overly paternalistic attitude on the part of the writers and compilers.

Nonetheless Sister Gleason does see some value in the positive findings. Through thesse literature texts the student would be exposed to minority characters displaying desirable traits which might have some significance in a society where minority group infractions are flagrantly publicized and noticc of accomplishments frequently muted in the public media. The one-sided literary picture may serve a positive function by merely balancing the usual public treatment, though one must wonder if this remains possible at present in light of the growing power of mass culture.

Some of the force of the positive orientation of the Catholic textbooks toward ethnic and racial groups evaporates once we recall the infrequent appearance of minority characters and references to racial-ethnic groups in these materials. The percentage of visibility for the black group category in the religion materials ranges from 2 percent to 8 percent. For the other ethnic groups the range extends from 1.7 percent to 19.6 percent. The total racial-ethnic percentage went from a low of 5.6 percent to a high of 31.2 percent.

However, many statements scored as positive for racial ethnic groups were extremely general, as may be seen from the following quotations taken from religion and social studies units:

(Religion) That noble document, the Declaration of Independence, proclaims that these truths are self-evident, "that all men are created equal, that they are endowed by their creator with certain inalienable rights, that among these are life, liberty, and the pursuit of happiness." These words admirably sum up the Christian teaching on human rights; they indicate the source of those rights, point out that no man may wantonly be deprived of them, and enumerate the most important ones.

(Religion) Christ's mystical body includes as actual or potential members the whole human race. And just as all men are thus united to Christ, so they are all united to one another by reason of this incorporation in his mystical body. This union is the most forceful reason for a man to treat all his fellow men with fraternal consideration.

(Social Studies) Our acceptance of others, our rights and obligations, are based on the principle of human solidarity. From the natural point of view, this solidarity is based on man's social nature. From the religious point of view, it is based on the truth that we all have a supernatural destiny and have been redeemed by the blood of Jesus Christ.

(Social Studies) Evidence of real progress toward the growth of an American Christian conscience lies in the recognition of the fundamental rights. Among these are the rights . . . of the Negro and the Indian to equal opportunities with the white man.

The frequency of general rather than specific references to racial-ethnic groups in the religion and social studies materials is a source of some concern. Given the orientation of the religion units, it might be argued that the general omission of references to specific racial-ethnic groups is largely due to the Catholic notion of the unity of all men in the body of Christ. Nonetheless, Sr. Thering expressed considerable dissatisfaction with the failure of the religion materials to treat the various racial-ethnic groups more comprehensively. Adolescents have a need for a constructive presentation of racial-ethnic relationships in specific rather than in general terms in order to answer the question: "Who is my neighbor?" An answer given in the specific environment of his pluralistic community will bring into open discussion the black man, the Mexican, the Puerto Rican, etc., his true brothers and sisters in Christ. Such treatment in the textbooks will clarify for the student the true significance of the teachings of the Hebrew Bible and the New Testament. Clarifications, instead of broad general clichés, will enable the student to fit himself into this picture of reality and offer him the opportunities to comprehend more fully what is really meant when he reads that he must love all men as he loves himself.

The lack of reference to racial and ethnic minorities in the social studies materials is even more disturbing. The vast majority of the texts devoted only from one to nine percent of their content to a treatment of Orientals, American Indians, blacks and Latin Americans. Several publications contained no references whatsoever to one or more of these groups.

With the emphasis on general rather than specific references to racial-ethnic groups in the religion materials and the "halo" treatment of minorities in much of the literature materials, the social studies texts become our chief source for an analysis of attitudes toward specific minorities. We will concentrate on the black man, the Indian, the Oriental, the Latin, the Jew and the "new immigrant."

THE BLACK MAN

On the positive side, the social studies units contained frequent descriptions of black people as acceptable citizens, friends and neighbors, as equal, not inferior, to others, and as skillful and contributing citizens who have participated courageously and effectively in our economic and social life. Positive statements placed emphasis on the contributions made by black people to our civilization—their achievements in the professions, in education, business, science and industry. Outstanding black men were credited with specific achievements and presented to the student as models of patriotism and industry. Major blame for the present situation of many black people in this country was attributed in several textbooks to white America. Segregation and discrimination in housing, education and recreation were deplored as serious blots on the American conscience. The Church also did not escape censure. While several textbooks indicated that the Catholic hierarchy in the United States had urged clergy and laity in 1866 to aid the black man, not much was done until the close of the century. The student was made aware that many Catholic institutions have followed a pattern of segregation and have failed generally to act in a Christian manner toward blacks. Occasionally, suspected student stereotypes of black people were attacked directly with corrective statements. Sister Rita Mudd pointed to such corrective statements as one of the best means available to counteract prejudice. In her view future instructional materials should make wider use of this tool which she felt was underemployed in the materials examined by her.

Following are some illustrations of positive references to the black group in the Catholic social studies materials.

The Negro was legally free [after the Civil War] but he was not prepared to use and enjoy his newly granted freedom. For a long time he found himself in a new kind of slavery at the hands of unscrupulous white men who exploited him but assumed no responsibility for him.

Negroes contributed to the prosperity of the South. . . . Their labor in the North has been of great economic value to the country. . . . Negroes have also contributed much to our native American literature, music and art, and the list of Negro inventors is an impressive one.

Unfortunately some Catholics have gone along with the pattern of segregation in churches, schools and hospitals.

We must face the fact that white Americans are largely responsible for the present-day plight of the Negro. Slavery, and then segregation and second class citizenship, brought on most of the evils which now beset our Negro neighbors.

There were virtually no statements in the textual materials that could be classified as explicitly negative. Negative implications constituted the chief reason for the researchers designating some statements as negative in tone. For example:

If Negroes in the South were given complete equality of educational and economic opportunity, what social problems would result? Can you suggest any way of eventually solving these problems in a gradual manner?

The examples given above show a definite awareness of the depth of the injustices done to black people in America. The problem is that such presentations were not frequent enough. Some improvement should also be made in the knowledge of the black man's contribution to American life as well as his African heritage. It is important for white students to know about some of the black Americans who have made a contribution to the total life of America, such as George Washington Carver, Ralph Bunche, and others. But it is equally vital for them to understand something about the internal history of the black community in America and the forces and figures that have influenced it. They should know who such men as Marcus Garvey, W. E. B. Du Bois and Martin Luther King were and what they stood for. High school students in particular should be presented with an explanation of the many and varied forms of segregation that continue to exist in our nation, and how the structure of ghetto life denies many opportunities to children. It is vital for the teacher to help the student go behind the external picture of ghetto life to the causes of the ghetto, some of which go back to the slavery era.

Teachers should also be careful to avoid that subtle form of racism which urges students to respect the black man because he "is really like us white people." In such an orientation the status and worth of minorities is judged by the degree to which they have adapted to the values and culture of the majority society. This caution applies as well to all the groups we are discussing in this chapter, not merely black people. Granted, in some respects this type of approach is partially inevitable. Also, from a Christian perspective, we do want to continue to stress the basic dignity and equality of all men. Yet we must constantly remind ourselves that, because we have not yet discovered the "universal man," nor found the way of adequately "stripping," as it were, universal manhood from its ethnic and racial concretizations, there is always the danger of identifying the true Christian man with the racial and ethnic group that predominates in a given society. While we certainly do not want to drive artificial wedges between peoples as we recall with St. Paul that as people in Christ we are ultimately neither Jew nor Gentile, we must recognize the continued value of diversity. Catholic students must learn to appreciate other peoples as much for their distinctive qualities and talents as for their sameness. For a teacher to bring together the poles of universality and diversity is admittedly not an easy task. But a proper understanding of the universality-diversity syndrome appears to be crucial to any successful resolution of the intergroup tension that is currently challenging our nation. Somehow we must adjust our ideal away from the former emphasis on societal assimilation toward one of shared diversity if our nation is to survive in a meaningful and human way.

THE AMERICAN INDIANS

Positive references to the Indian group and its contributions to American life were, on the whole, not as frequent as for the Negro group. Furthermore, there were many more examples of expressly negative statements with respect to Indians. Some of the textual materials did criticize our attempts to force the American Indian into our common cultural and social patterns. Some entries described the Indians as the "first families of America," and as friendly, brave and kind people. Other statements referred to the Indian as progressive and devoted to his family. Receiving high praise were the rich Indian legacy of native arts, music and handicrafts as well as the group's abilities in hunting, fishing and farming. The authors of several publications clearly told the student that our nation has failed to recognize the dignity and rights of the Indian population of America. Our Indian policies were termed the "seamy side of our democracy," "the worst blot on the story of our expansion," and "a chapter of dishonor." The following are typical of the positive textbook references to Indians:

Surely the Indians were brave men, too. They showed heroic courage against their enemies in the face of cold, hunger, and torture.

The Southwest Indians were very progressive. They were good farmers. They built dams and dug ditches to irrigate the dry, sandy land. They excelled, too, in weaving, pottery, and the making of baskets.

The United States owes much to the Indians. . . . The American Indians taught us the use of the tomato, maize, potato, and other agricultural products, and their art and folk tales have likewise enriched our culture.

The treatment of the Indians in the American states and territories showed that self-interest and not high principles were behind the actions of individuals and the government. . . . They [the frontiersmen] did not admit that the native Indians, who had possessed the land in the first place, had any right to it at all. The treatment of the Indian by the white man in the United States does not make pleasant reading. "A century of dishonor" is perhaps not too harsh a term to use in describing it.

Negative stereotyping of the Indian group was also found in the textbooks:

The Indians were fickle and unreliable.

The Indians were the racial group which made the fewest positive contributions to the national development.

They [Indians] had the cruel ways that always go with pagan beliefs.

A ceremonial dance by New Mexico Indians (illustrated by a picture). Dancing plays a large part in the culture of many backward people.

The Blackfoot Indians of Montana never stopped looking for revenge.

On the whole the portrait of the Indian group that emerges from the St. Louis studies is not as encouraging as that of the black American. And because the Indian population is considerably smaller than that of the black population and not generally situated in the major urban areas, little is being done to counteract the strongly distorted image of the American Indian in the various media, television in particular. Most students have probably never met an Indian in person. Their picture of the Indian is frequently still that of the American Western which continues to be propagated in films and on television. The slum conditions under which many blacks are forced to live are more easily visible to the average student than the conditions of poverty which Indians are often forced to accept on reservations. Our image of the Indian is still largely the romantic one of a Tonto or the savage one of the Wild West villain.

Precisely because the possibility of improving the portrait of the Indian through the mass media and existential contact is much more limited than for the black American, the classroom becomes doubly important as a corrective vehicle. The diverse cultures of American Indians must become better known to students as well as their present and past exploitation by white America. There should also be some awareness of self-improvement developments among the Indians. Students need to understand why Indians feel a present need to bolster group identity to overcome the alienation they have experienced from the majority white society of European heritage. Some of them look to the Jewish community, as do some of the blacks, for a model to follow.[1] The Jewish sense of peoplehood has become attractive to both Indians and blacks in America.

Robert W. Rietz, director of the American Indian Center in Chicago, is emphatic in insisting that the Indian has been tragically overlooked by American society. "The teaching of Indian history," he says, "is less than pathetic. The entire Indian removal policy of federal administrations during the nineteenth century is unmentioned. Nowhere do young people really learn about the development of the reservation system. Just think of it—extermination, reservations. Yet nothing in our textbooks."[2]

Mr. Rietz maintains that a study of the contemporary American Indian can provide several worthwhile lessons for the entire urban majority: (1) the urban Indian is showing that traditional group values can be maintained in the midst of an impersonal, increasingly uniform and often hostile environment; (2) the Indian is proving that social welfare programs can be effectively administered by the recipient groups without the need for rigid bureaucratic direction; and (3) the Indian is displaying to the non-

Indian population the importance of each individual having a feeling of kinship with the community, of belonging to a larger organic group that embraces all.

In addition to the native American Indian, students should be exposed to the history and cultures of the various Indian civilizations that have existed in both North and South America. Our treatment of Latin America is generally poor. But our treatment of the native Indian populations of such countries as Mexico and Peru is even worse. It is almost totally non-existent. The same applies to an awareness of the situation of the Eskimos and Aleuts in the state of Alaska.

ORIENTALS

Oriental peoples, whether American or Asian, received only scant consideration in the textbooks examined by the St. Louis research staff. Omission once again was the major source of criticism. What material there was on Orientals generally attained a favorable evaluation, although a few entries in the literature materials implied that Orientals were dishonest. There were occasional references to the Oriental group which highlighted the rich civilizations in such countries as China long before Western civilization had begun to develop. Oriental contributions to civilization generally, such as pottery, porcelain, paper, tea, glass, ink and printing, also received some acknowledgment. Stress was placed in a few instances on the beauty and dignity of Oriental religious and cultural life, philosophy, music and art. The following textbook entries illustrate this approach:

Beauty is a daily necessity to the Japanese, and love of beauty is a part of the soul of every man, woman and child. Japanese artists paint beautiful pictures, make exquisite lacquers and pottery, and erect graceful buildings, but that is not all. Even the simplest things of everyday life are made beautiful with a sure touch and natural good taste.

In spite of political changes the religious and cultural life of China developed to a high state while Western Europe was still struggling with barbarism.

A common criticism hurled at these people of Southern and Eastern Asia is that they adhere rigidly to an ancient culture. It is necessary to realize that these Orientals are the best judges of what is noble and honorable in their culture. What suits one part of the world will not necessarily suit another. We owe much to these people. Many devices and inventions common now in the West can be traced back to Asian origin. The Japanese and Chinese in particular have influenced our culture.

The Chinese helped to build many of our railroads. Economic discrimination has kept them in rather limited occupations, such as restaurant and laundry work. Housing discrimination has segregated them in over-populated areas.

Several authors referred to discrimination against Chinese people in the San Francisco school system, to the herding of Americans of Japanese descent into closed-off detention camps during World War II, and to the rigid immigration restrictions against people from Asian lands.

The textbooks examined by the St. Louis research team did not contain much explicitly negative material about Orientals. (A possible exception might be the fact that the Mongoloid group headed the list of illiterate characters in most of the literature series.) As with many of the other minorities, omission is the most serious accusation that has to be leveled against the treatment of Oriental peoples, whether Americans or Asians.

To rectify this situation in the future, teachers will need to begin inculcating in their students some awareness of the great Oriental cultures and civilizations, past and present. Special emphasis might very well be placed on the Oriental influence in our own state of Hawaii. In general, an improvement in our presentation of the Oriental peoples will demand expanding the traditional preoccupation in our history and social studies courses with Western European and native American history. Events and cultures from other parts of the world have received a shabby treatment at best. They were usually brought in only when Europeans or Americans were involved there in wars or colonial expansion. Our students learn much about the China of the Boxer Rebellion days, for example, but virtually nothing about the more creative periods in the long and proud history of Chinese civilization. Finally, some effort should be made to cut through some of the romantic notions many white Americans have about the life that awaits the Chinese American in the Chinatowns of San Francisco, Chicago, New York or elsewhere. Behind the glitter of the tourist shops and restaurants we will find problems in housing, education, working conditions and social services because of past discrimination and neglect. Students should come to know that the Chinese were brought to this country originally to construct our railroad system, that they were never adequately compensated for their arduous work, and that little was done to prepare them for successful integration into the majority society.

THE LATIN PEOPLES

The Latin American group in this country received very little attention as a whole in the textual materials. Puerto Rican and Mexican-Americans are mentioned on occasion as Spanish-speaking immigrants who have been subject to considerable discrimination in the United States. Virtually nothing, however, is said about their culture. On the other hand, the researchers discovered substantial content which spoke in a positive vein of the peoples in Latin America itself. These references stressed the deep-seated culture of the Latin peoples, the strength of their family life and their friendly and courteous attitudes. Pan-Americanism was emphasized and put forth as an ideal by many of the textbook authors. Students were told that a spirit of hemispheric unity would prove beneficial to all the countries of South and North America. One social studies publication depicted Pan-Americanism as an ideal developed after World War II which has helped to bring about a better understanding and appreciation of Latin American culture and has encouraged a more favorable view of Latin Americans among North Americans. The various Pan-American meetings held through the years have, the textbooks allege, prevented many of the misunderstandings that foster friction among nations. "Mutual friendship promotes peace" was a common theme of the authors.

Other entries told the student that the Pan-American union is awakening the peoples of North and South America to the advantages of better understanding among its members, that the Good Neighbor policy was a source of strength, and that the Organization of American States and the Institute of Inter-American Affairs have done much to promote a better life for the peoples of South America and mutual understanding among all the peoples of the hemisphere. Several of the authors clearly brought out the unjust conditions under which Mexicans are forced to work in our country, while others criticized aspects of our policies toward Latin nations, especially during the presidency of Theodore Roosevelt. There was also an attempt by a few of the textbooks to directly attack suspected student stereotypes of Latins. The following typify the statements which form the Latin American portrait in the textbooks:

The people in those countries [Latin America] had fought for their freedom just as we had, and most of them had adopted constitutions modeled after ours.

These people have developed a fine religious heritage and a deep-seated culture. Family life is strong; divorce and juvenile delinquency are almost unknown.

While Mexicans are seasonally employed in the United States in large numbers, they do not always share the advantages of wages or favorable working conditions with American workers. This prompts the need for the passage of laws that oppose injustice to any workers.

Unfortunately the Mexican War and Theodore Roosevelt's methods in securing the land for the Panama Canal made the Latin American states very mistrustful of Yankee imperialism.

Many think that the people [Latin Americans] are still backward and unprogressive. Yet in many ways they are extremely modern and progressive, and boast of unusual cultural and educational facilities.

41

Despite these genuinely positive comments, the portrait of the Latin American group in Catholic instructional materials is open to several criticisms. One is shallowness of treatment. There is really very little offered the student in the way of a sympathetic presentation of the genius of the great Latin American civilizations that have been formed out of the Indian, Spanish, Portuguese and Moorish components. Most American students know virtually nothing about the history of the countries in Latin America, not even that of Mexico and our immediate neighbors to the south, except when those countries have somehow entered directly the history of the United States (e.g., Mexican War, Panama Canal, Spanish-American War, etc.). (The same is true incidentally for the history of our neighbor to the north, Canada.) This is only another example of our excessive preoccupation with Western European and American history.

Very little is also said of the situation of the Latin minorities in our own country, either about the very real hardships and the discrimination they have experienced, or about the rich Spanish culture of the Southwest and parts of Florida. Rarely is much attention given to the fact that two of our oldest cities, Santa Fe and St. Augustine, are Spanish in origin. Likewise little is presented about the commonwealth of Puerto Rico, its development, and its past and present relationship to the federal government.

But over and above the omissions, we must also recognize definite distortions in some of the textbook materials which stress the so-called spirit of Pan Americanism. While a few authors tried to point out to the student the real injustices that have marked our policy toward Latin American nations, the greater number of entries left the student with the impression that we have generally exhibited a real sense of concern and respect for their peoples. Unfortunately the situation is almost the exact opposite. A true Pan-American spirit has been the exception rather than the rule in our dealings with Latin America.[3] This applies as well to the Organization of American States which is deeply discredited in much of Latin America. Even the best of our approaches such as President Franklin Roosevelt's Good Neighbor Policy have had serious shortcomings in spite of the fact that the Good Neighbor

Policy constituted a real light in a history of our relations with the peoples to the south of us, a history in which we have little cause for pride. Students must begin to understand that even so-called "foreign aid" has frequently hurt the Latin economy far more than it has helped it, while at the same time it proved of great benefit to our own fiscal well-being. Without a greater awareness by Americans of the past injustices perpetrated by our nation against Latin America we can never hope for any real reconciliation among the peoples of our hemisphere.

The poverty and suffering of so much of Latin America is staggering and difficult to justify for any sensitive Christian. Because of the special relationship between the United States and Latin America the alleviation of these desperate conditions depends in large part on our nation. While still presenting our students with the potential inherent in the ideals of our country, we must try to make them aware of the serious failures of our foreign policy relative to Latin Americans. To shrink from this serious responsibility would be false patriotism and false Christianity. It is a challenging and sensitive assignment for teachers to handle.

THE JEWISH GROUP

Although we will take up the textbook findings regarding Jews in a later chapter, some mention of them in this chapter on racial and ethnic groups is important because Judaism is not just a religious phenomenon. Jews combine both an ethnic and a religious aspect around a common core of peoplehood, and this facet of Judaism is probably the one Christians find most difficult to grasp. The textbooks examined seldom developed this aspect of Jewish life. Their presentations, whether prejudiced or enlightened, generally concentrated on the religious aspects of Judaism, only occasionally mentioning persecution of Jews in countries and centuries other than our own.

Regarding this serious gap in Christian historical materials, Edward Flannery has commented:

Jews generally are acutely aware of the history of anti-Semitism, simply because it comprises so large a portion of Jewish history. Christians, on the contrary, even highly educated ones, are all but totally ignorant of it—except for contemporary developments. They are ignorant of it for the simple reason that anti-Semitism does not appear in their history books. Histories of the Middle Ages—and even of the Crusades—can be found in which the word "Jew" does not appear, and there are Catholic dictionaries and encyclopedias in which the term "anti-Semitism" is not listed. There seems to be only one conclusion: The pages Jews have memorized have been torn from our histories of the Christian era.[4]

What is needed to advance our understanding of Jews (as with the other groups discussed in this chapter) is some sense of their continuous experience as a distinct people, including both the achievements and the difficulties they have encountered. For American Jews this would mean some description of the various Jewish migrations to the U.S., how they were forced into certain social and ethnic patterns in this country (the source of many of the common Gentile stereotypes of Jews), and how they were the target of social and economic discrimination. These patterns of discrimination against Jews are in part responsible for some of the anti-Jewish feelings in black ghetto communities. The most visible and indentifiable white presence there is often the small Jewish merchant, while Gentiles have practiced discrimination far more serious behind the walls of large, impersonal corporations.

Skillful use of literature may be one helpful way of providing Christian students with some insight into the internal experience of Jews.[5] Msgr. John Oesterreicher of the Institute of Judaeo-Christian Studies at Seton Hall University even sees great instructional possibilities in such an apparently anti-Jewish play as Shakespeare's "The Merchant of Venice."

As you well know, one of Shakespeare's great plays, "The Merchant of Venice," is a stumbling block for many. There are Christians as well as Jews who would like to see it taken off the curriculum or consider its performance by the drama club of any school taboo. I am not one of them. As a matter of fact, I think it a perfect means for transmitting this sensitivity. It is not a play hostile to *Jews;* rather does it castigate Christians *and* Jews, that is to say, the sinfulness of man.

Not a single character in the play is a person of moral integrity. Antonio, for instance, appears to be a man of noble heart, kind and unselfish; in reality he is no less a seeker after profit than Shylock. The difference is that Shylock's business is despised, whereas Antonio's is praised. Yet, even the praise discloses its metal: "where your argosies with portly sail . . . do overpeer the petty traffickers" (I, i, 9, 12). There seems to be so little difference between the big trader and the money lender that, at the end of the play, Portia—disguised as a young lawyer—can ask: "Which is the merchant, and which the Jew?" (IV, i, 174). The arrogance and hypocrisy of the Christians of the play are most obvious at the elopement of Lorenzo with Jessica. Before she is ready to join her lover, she returns to the house for some more money to take with her. When Gratiano hears her resolve to add theft to the betrayal of her father, he says: "Now by my hood, a Gentile, and no Jew" (II, vi, 51). These Christians, whose faith is no more than skin deep, welcome Jessica's "conversion," but she does not turn to Christ—Christ is not even mentioned—she only wishes to escape the boredom of her home and her father's shame in the world of glitter.

The climax of hypocrisy is the little drama in the court of justice. What some will take to be Portia's noble attempt at saving Bassanio is, to her, little more than a prank. (The affair with the ring confirms her as a practical joker.) She plays her role well. For a moment, she even surpasses herself and grows ecstatic. Her rapturous praise of mercy reaches evangelical heights; yet, her whole line of defense is meant to trick Shylock. He leaves the court ill. He is given this choice: either he becomes a Christian (IV, i, 387) —or presently he must die! Need I add that this is an utter travesty of everything Christian? Though Shylock lives, his spirit is broken, his will crushed. Without faith, he is forced to become a Christian—and all this by the champion of mercy. As I see it, "The Merchant of Venice" is far from being an anti-Jewish play; it is, rather, an unmasking of all sham Christians. It could be a textbook for Christian-Jewish relations; it condenses a millennium to the life of one generation. If taught with discretion or played with sensitivity, it would convey to the student or spectator the sins of Christendom and implant in him the desire to make amends, to turn the conciliar Statement on the Jews into a living reality.[6]

Special sensitivity is required in the use of literary sources to round out the Jewish portrait for Christian students. As Solomon Liptin points out in his book *The Jews in American Literature,* the Jewish portrait has been shaped by a number of conflicting tendencies: Protestant veneration of the Hebrew patriarchs, the liberal spirit of the Enlightenment, and the "evil Jew" stereotype, a part of Western tradition whose prototype was Judas and who gained prominence in European drama and fiction via the mystery play, Chaucer, Marlowe and Shakespeare.

In spite of many differences, the struggles of the Jewish immigrant community to adjust to American life, as reflected in the literary record, may provide insights to the situation of other minority groups. Many Christian Americans have been reluctant, and still are, to grant Jews full equality in the benefits of American life. As a result, a certain segment of the Jewish population— and here fiction seems to faithfully reflect reality—was inclined to cast aside all vestiges of its Jewish origins and to try to make itself indistinguishable from the majority of American society. Others, however, discovered or rediscovered their Jewish heritage, having undergone the often painful experience that complete assimilation was both an impossible dream and a betrayal of their true identity as Jews.

The struggle to be found in Jewish literature between the poles of complete assimilation and ethnic identity may well have raised the first profound challenge to the American melting pot concept. It also revealed the psychological destructiveness of self-hatred. In challenging the melting pot concept, Jews also uncovered the limitations of American "universalism."

In spite of our claims, America was and still is essentially a white Christian country. "White" and "Christian" have been inseparably linked. Jews have had trouble because they were not Christians, even though they are white. Other groups, despite their Christian faith, have had difficulty because they were non-white or only "peripherally" white from the viewpoint of a Western European white society. This holds true for American blacks (a great many of whom were Baptists) and Spanish-Americans.

Literature is thus a good method of introducing a student on both knowledge and feeling levels to the situation of the Jew in American society. In particular, literature can give the student a good awareness of what life has been like for the Jew in this country. It would be shortsighted to concentrate solely on the religious aspects of Judaism in treating of the Jewish people. Their role as an American minority group also deserves adequate consideration by the teacher.

THE "NEW IMMIGRANTS"

To conclude this chapter we will take up an aspect of intergroup relations in America brought out only in the literature study. There was no parallel category for the New Immigrants in either the religion or social studies analyses. Basically this category involves a distinction between the presentation of the Old Immigrant group, the "builders of our nation," and the portrait of the New Immigrants such as Italians, Poles, Russians, Greeks, etc., who came to America in great numbers after 1880. The results of the literature study indicate that the textbook authors and compilers identified the Old Immigrants as the "we" group, while the New Immigrants were looked upon as the "they" group. The Old Immigrants had considerably more representation in major speaking roles and they ranked higher in honesty, educational status, respectability and desirability. The only category in which the New Immigrants held a slight advantage was prudence. But this situation may actually be interpreted as something less than complimentary in the overall portrait of the New Immigrants. It may actually be a subtle way of emasculating the New Immigrant group.

The situation of the New Immigrant group in America has taken on a renewed importance in the current American social situation. Many members of this group (especially the Slavic peoples) are only beginning to reach full acceptance in American society. A good number of them in the past tried to disguise their origins in the same manner as some Jews through such devices as changing their surnames. Many of the New Immigrant group may still not feel totally at home in the American social environment. They may continue to believe that in some ways they have not as yet been fully incorporated into the mainstream of American life. And it is frequently these New Immigrant peoples that stand in the way of the advancement of other minorities such as blacks and Spanish-Americans. It is important that students be given some insights into the situation of the New Immigrant groups. They should also acquire some knowledge of the history and culture of their ancestral countries, something that has been by-passed in our study of European history up till now, with the emphasis almost totally on Western Europe. Such a presentation of the situation of the New Immigrant group in America is of special importance for Catholic students. A great many of them are descendants of this group. A realistic knowledge of their situation past and present may help to lessen some of the intergroup problems now existing between the New Immigrant group and our advancing minority groups. This lack of full assimilation of the New Immigrants is a factor that has not been given adequate expression in many of the recent analyses of the sources of social tension in our country.

FOOTNOTES

1. Cf. *Report of the 1968 International Conference of Christians and Jews,* York University, Toronto, Canada, September 2-6, 1968, p. 33. The black man's identification with the Jewish experience can be found in the writings of Malcolm X (despite his occasional hostility toward the Jewish people) and in Albert Cleage, *The Black Messiah,* New York: Sheed and Ward, 1969.
2. *The Christian Science Monitor,* November 20, 1968, p. 8.
3. Cf. John Gerassi, *The Great Fear in Latin America,* New York: Macmillan, 1965.
4. Edward H. Flannery, *op. cit.,* p. xi.
5. Cf. Sister Louis Gabriel, "The Jew in American Literature," SIDIC, No. 2, 1969, pp. 9-14 and Monsignor John M. Oesterreicher, *Shalom: The Encounter of Christians and Jews and the Catholic Educator,* South Orange, N.J.: Institute of Judaeo-Christian Studies, Seton Hall University.
6. John M. Oesterreicher, *op. cit.,* pp. 8-9.
7. New York: Bloch Publishing Co., 1966.

CHAPTER 4

THE PORTRAITS OF
NON-CATHOLIC RELIGIOUS GROUPS

The St. Louis studies reveal no consistent pattern in the portraits of the religious outgroups which concern us in this chapter: Protestants, Eastern Orthodox, Eastern rite Catholics, and non-Christians.* The social studies textbooks gave the most positive orientation to these groups. Though lower than the corresponding scores for racial-ethnic groups, the scores for religious outgroups stand at a very respectable level of 72 percent positive for the sum total of references to Protestants and 89 percent positive for references to non-Christian groups. Moreover, the social studies units frequently stressed the need for acceptance of all religions, highlighted beliefs shared in common, and urged inter-religious cooperation in civic affairs and on issues involving public morality. The textbooks invoked both secular (the American spirit of toleration) and religious (the fatherhood of God as the foundation of the unity of mankind) authoritative traditions in urging harmony and decrying religious bigotry. Some illustrative examples from

*The term "non-Christians" is sometimes used as a broad, generalized category in the textbooks. References to Buddhism, Confucianism, etc. also fell into this category. Except for the literature study, which included Jewish references under "non-Christian," it does *not* refer to Jews.

the social studies textbooks:

> Our teaching on the family, on morality in public and business life, on race relations and on international unity, to mention but a few points stressed in these pages, is accepted by many who are not Catholics. Nearly all our teachings in these fields are shared by . . . Protestants and Jews. Many of these ideals are based on the natural law and would be professed by men of good will, no matter what their religious belief.

> More and more, Catholic leaders have shown a disposition to co-operate with Protestant and Jewish leaders in civic questions wherein all share a common moral principle. They have frequently found themselves taking a common stand on certain measures affecting the rights of the working class, immigration, and similar matters that have direct moral implications.

> Christ was not a separatist; he went about doing good and did not allow artificial barriers to circumscribe his mission.

> In nations where persons of different religious beliefs live side by side, charity is necessary if peace and friendship are to pervade the body politic. Tolerance, forbearance, respect for the honest convictions of others, all dictated by charity, will eliminate ill will and bigotry. Nothing disturbs natural unity so much as religious bigotry, which at base is due to lack of charity. Charity obliges us to accord the same measure of freedom of conscience to others that we demand for ourselves and those of our religious belief.

> We are happy because so many people pray to God, in so many places near and far away. We love all these people, and remember that they are God's children. They are like our sisters and brothers because God is our Father.

The literature units do not reveal as positive an orientation toward religious outgroups as was found in the social studies materials. Here the picture is much more confused, with some materials portraying non-Catholics in a fairly favorable light, while other series cast them in roles that definitely make them inferior to Catholic characters.

In the literature materials, the religious affiliation of nearly 60 percent of the characters was uncertain. In the three series compiled specifically for Catholic school use, Catholic characters predominated. In the set compiled for general use, but adopted by many Catholic schools, non-Catholic Christian groups had the strongest representation. In contrast to the first three series where Catholics comprised an average of 21.7 percent of the total speaking characters and 52.6 percent of the religiously identifiable characters, Catholics formed only 9.7 percent of all speaking characters and 27 percent of religiously identifiable characters in the non-Catholic series. Non-Christian characters averaged 1.2 percent of the total speaking characters in all sets.

The visibility scores for non-Christians in the literature study suggest that silence, rather than overt negativism, is the problem. Obviously in textbooks written for Christian students in a society basically rooted in Christian culture, the predominance of Christian characters comes as no great surprise and hardly deserves criticism. It is similarly understandable that Catholics, themselves a minority, would choose compilations of literature which highlight the contributions of their own group or include a higher proportion of Catholic characters than would be found in general anthologies. But in times when we have increasing contacts as a people with non-Christian religious traditions, it would seem important to ensure that students be exposed to literary materials in which the presence of identifiable non-Christian characters would be greater than a meager 1.2 percent. Ten percent would be much more of an acceptable minimum.

The religious textbooks, as might be expected, showed a high preoccupation with other religions. Nevertheless, there existed great disparity in the amount of space devoted to specific religious outgroups. Very few units, for example, contained any material on Eastern rite Catholics. And the treatment of non-Catholic groups frequently occurred only when these groups appeared on the scene chronologically in Catholic history as a schismatic or heretical group. Most of the publishers did receive an overall positive score for their treatment of religious outgroups. But some of the examples of positively scored references cited below strike one as paternalistic by today's standards.

Now not only Catholics but non-Catholics as well can attain to the state of grace. For instance, a non-Catholic who, by an act of perfect love or perfect contrition, has received baptism of desire,

51

is united to Christ by an invisible bond as long as he persists in the state of grace.

Non-Catholics who, through no fault of their own, do not know that the Catholic Church is the true Church, may be pleasing to God. The Catholic teaching that "outside the Church there is no salvation" does not mean that everyone who is not a Catholic will be damned. It means that salvation comes to men in and through the Catholic Church. Therefore, non-Catholics who are in the state of grace, are in the Catholic Church, though invisibly, and if they persevere in grace, they will be saved.

It is quite possible, however, for a Protestant to be "in good faith" in holding to some truths and rejecting others, for he may not know that these others are revealed. If he knew, he would accept them.

Excerpts from two different textbooks illustrate how the same theme (in this case, the mystical body) can be treated both positively and negatively:

Christ really wants all to be members of his mystical body, and everyone is thus potentially, if not actually, a member. For this reason we have charity for all persons. Race, nationality, position, personality—all these things must be brushed aside by the life that Christ wants to bind all people together in him.

Many Protestants are baptized but as they do not accept the Catholic faith, they do not belong to the mystical body. The Orthodox church members are baptized and they profess most of the truth of the faith taught by the Catholic Church; their refusal to give obedience to the pope, however, excludes them from the mystical body.

The visibility of the non-Christian religious group in the religion materials was rather low, ranging from 4.3 percent to a high of 12.5 percent. The portrait of non-Christians was generally positive, but the scores were not especially impressive. A negative reference is illustrated below:

There are many non-Christian sects who do not believe in the Trinity and therefore do not accept Christ as divine. Among these are the Universalists, Unitarians, Christian Scientists, Jews, Mohammedans, Buddhists, unconverted pagans, and many so-called "scientists," "evolutionists," "materialists" and "rationalists" who trust too much in their poor feeble reason and refuse the guidance of faith and the Church. Pray for all unbelievers and help them by word, and work to find the Church.

A consideration of the presentation of non-Catholic groups in the religion materials must leave the sensitive Christian teacher with some feelings of deep disappointment. That the social studies materials presented religious outgroups in a fairer and more balanced way than did the religion materials raises uneasy questions about what we have been presenting to our Catholic students in religion texts over the years. An examination of references to the specific outgroups mentioned in the St. Louis studies makes it abundantly clear that the religion textbooks provide the most serious problems.

PROTESTANT CHRISTIANS

As indicated, the social studies units offered the student a fairly positive picture of Protestantism. References to Protestants fell into three basic categories: (1) those mentioning the Reformation; (2) entries concerned with early Protestant colonists in America; and (3) those dealing with later developments in America and present-day activities.

Statements within the first of these categories, the Protestant Reformation, were least numerous, but frequently emphasized the abuses and weaknesses existing in the Church at the time of Martin Luther, as well as the political, social and cultural causes of the Reformation. On occasion the textual materials spoke of the "true and religious zeal in the minds of many who broke with Rome."

Luther was presented by some of the textbook authors as a man of talent and ability whose criticism of the Church had some validity:

In the year 1517, Luther attacked some practices that had grown

53

up in the Church in regard to indulgences. These practices were not approved by the officials of the Church and Luther had a right to criticize them. But Luther soon went on to deny some of the chief teachings of the Church.

About twenty German translations of the Bible had appeared before his time, but the beauty of Luther's version made it very popular, and it had great influence upon the development of the modern German language.

Here [University of Wittenberg] Luther distinguished himself as a forceful and eloquent preacher and teacher.

John Calvin, another Reformation leader, was described by one of the texts as a man of great learning and intellect who in 1536 published the monumental *Institutes of the Christian Religion.*

Speaking of the Catholic Church in colonial times and the difficulties she faced as a minority group, many of the publications stressed that despite the considerable injustices suffered by Catholics there were many honest, fair-minded Protestants who disapproved of the unjust laws which deprived Catholics of religious freedom, voting rights and public office. Special mention was made of the freedom accorded Catholics by William Penn in Pennsylvania and Roger Williams in Rhode Island.

Pennsylvania did not pass laws against Catholics. The Quakers were sympathetic toward them, and in fact there were a number of Irish teachers in Pennsylvania, many of whom were Catholics.

Even though Pennsylvania became the center of Quaker life, Catholics, too, were welcomed. Anyone who believed in God could live there. They enjoyed freedom in the practice of their religion. They shared in the friendly government of the Quakers.

The outstanding leader of these people [colony of Rhode Island] was Roger Williams, a charitable Puritan preacher. . . . Roger Williams was an extremely tolerant leader.

In the post-colonial period Protestants were frequently singled out for their positive influence on the American character, for their social services in behalf of youth and education, and for their general service to the nation by preserving moral values and contributing to the solution of social problems.

American religious life showed great vitality. Protestantism, which dominated the religious scene [during the period of Jeffersonian Republicanism], revealed vigor in expansion, organization and thought.

The YMCA is typical of the Protestant interest in social service.

This [the Federal Council of Churches] illustrated a notable tendency in American Protestantism to take an active interest in social, economic, and political affairs in which moral questions were involved.

Several textbooks clearly acknowledged the deficiencies in the Catholic Church, especially in the period when the Protestant reform began. The authors spoke openly of the immorality, selfishness and ignorance of some members of the clergy, including the popes, in Luther's day. Other textbooks criticized Catholic persecutions of Protestants in the past as a serious violation of "freedom of conscience" and as a cruel and intolerable action.

By the sixteenth century the papacy was all too frequently more interested in petty Italian politics than in overcoming corruption.

Many of the clergy became worldly, and politics became amoral if not immoral. These conditions ultimately led to the division of the Christian world, commonly known as the Protestant Revolt.

It is true that reform was needed. The Catholic Church, despite her divine mission, has never claimed that her members cannot sin. Even popes have been found imperfect and weak, going so far in some instances as to misuse their high position to further personal interests. . . . The Church has never claimed to be perfect, in clergy or members. . . . The Church needs reform at all times in her members and never tires of preaching it. She needed it in the sixteenth century more than in any other period of her history.

But the presentation of Protestants in the social studies materials is by no means totally free of negative content. The following references illustrate some of the negative statements:

Luther: cruel, twisted childhood. Sentimental, torn between fear of God and the love of sensual pleasure. Calvin: severe, narrow, hypocritical. Ambitious for power and rule. Proud and fanatical.

The Scottish nobility, moved by greed for the Church's riches and inspired by fanatical Calvinist John Knox, turned Scotland Protestant.

Martin Luther, the first and foremost revolutionary, openly taught not charity, purity, and humility, but hatred, vulgarity, and senseless pride. His conduct closely followed his teaching.

The Protestant Revolt led to bitter intolerance and war; it led to an intensification of nationalism, the capitalistic spirit, absolutism, and secularization.

The Protestant Revolution against the Catholic Church in the sixteenth century spread fanaticism and intolerance, and was the main cause of many wars for more than a century.

Unlike many Protestant sects, the Catholic body, true to the social principles of Christ, was not split by the knife of sectional discord and racial prejudice. . . . This unity impressed many non-Catholics.

As previously mentioned, the religion materials' approach to non-Catholic groups was heavily negative in tone. Protestants were the second most visible group in the religion materials and the group most negatively portrayed. Hostile references to the Protestant group in the religion materials clustered around three areas: (1) doctrinal differences with the Roman Catholic Church; (2) the Reformation; and (3) areas of modern Catholic-Protestant conflict (e.g., Protestant missions in Latin America).

Author William Clancy, recalling his own experience as a student, is quoted pointedly by Sister Thering:

In the primary and secondary schools, I learned the standard things, all negative: Protestants reject the authority of the pope; they do not honor the Virgin; they deny the efficacy of good works; they acknowledge only two sacraments, etc. . . . Through

56

eighteen years of Catholic education I heard nothing positive about Protestantism. No teacher ever suggested that beyond the Reformation's negations, Protestantism has a prophetic vision of its own.[1]

Representative excerpts from the religion materials exemplify this approach:

Protestantism granted concessions in an attempt to attack all who lacked courage to live up to the high standard proposed by Christ and the Church. Protestantism today is rapidly deteriorating, while the unchanging spiritual Church has grown ever stronger with the years.

What conclusion can be drawn from the fact that the only point of unity among Protestants is opposition to the Catholic Church?

In the sixteenth and seventeenth centuries, the Protestant Revolt divided the defenders of the supernatural into two hostile camps, with the result that most of the sects which broke away from the Church have since lost all sense of the supernatural, and have frankly worked to spread secularism even into the field of religion.

On the inside the Church has always had a certain number of proud people called "heretics" who seem to think they know more about God's business than God himself. The latest of these, those who called themselves Protestant Reformers, are realizing more and more, as time goes on, that the Church was right. Every census in the United States shows a gain for the Catholics and a decrease for almost all the others.

After four hundred years of starvation without most of the sacraments, non-Catholics today have grown to view man in an opposite way; now they hardly think of him as anything more than an animal.

Luther's unrestrained passions led him to sin, and in his pride he refused to have his life be considered sin. He worked out, therefore, a different teaching, in which the ideas of sin and of goodness were changed to correspond to what it pleased him at the time to consider sin or virtue. His pleasure, rather than truth, was to be the standard for measuring right and wrong.

No one will deny that Catholic views of the Reformation will differ from Protestant interpretations and that the Catholic viewpoint will involve some critical judgment of the Protestant position (as a Protestant viewpoint will involve some critical assessment of the Catholic approach). The kind of distortion which characterizes the above excerpts needs to be avoided, however, as well as the use of pejorative descriptions such as those from a Church history text describing various leaders of the Reformation as "obstinate heretics," "self-satisfied monarch," "positively immoral," "drunken brewer," and "adulterous tyrant."

While there is room for disagreement between Protestants and Catholics on many issues, the textbooks examined in the St. Louis study frequently contained unfair implications that Protestant groups are Christian in name only and do not actually try to live in accord with the teachings of the New Testament. For example:

A Christian is a baptized person who believes the teachings of Jesus Christ and lives according to them. . . . Many call themselves Christians although they believe only part of the teachings of Christ. Such Christians are Lutherans, Methodists, Episcopalians, and other Protestants, as well as members of the Orthodox church. Strictly speaking, Catholics are the only real Christians, as they believe all the teachings of Christ and try to live according to them.

The same type of distortion appeared on occasion in textbook discussions of modern-day conflicts between Catholics and Protestants. The following two passages, from two different textbook series, are representative of the tone found in such prejudiced discussions:

Protestantism and Communism have hindered the Catholic Church in South America. Although Protestants, mostly from the United States, have not won many converts from Catholicism, they have succeeded in making some Catholics indifferent to their faith. Their vast financial resources also threaten to weaken the respect for the Church in areas where they can supply much needed help for the poor.

Besides local problems, Catholics of Latin American countries face two sources of trouble from the outside: Communists and American Protestants. . . . The Protestants, supported by plentiful funds from the United States, are still attempting to "convert" Latin American Catholics, a procedure that has frequently caused the latter to look upon all North American help as treachery in disguise.

There has been substantial improvement in the portrait of Protestant groups since the time of the St. Louis studies. Protestant-Catholic rapprochement has advanced further than any other aspect of the ecumenical movement. Much of the hostility and triumphalism is gone, partly as a result of the studies themselves. But Catholics should not lull themselves into a false sense of total accomplishment. As a person active in ecumenical work on the popular level, I continue to hear many of the same negative attitudes contained in the "old" textbooks verbalized again and again by Catholics, including Catholic teachers. Hence, the following recommendations with respect to the presentation of Protestantism to Catholic students need to be taken seriously by teachers.

On many points of belief a Catholic-Protestant polarization is no longer fully accurate. Certain Catholics may feel closer to certain Protestants on some issues than to their fellow Catholics, and vice versa. Students should be aware of this. We must also eliminate from our instructional materials any residue of the old attitudes toward Luther and the Protestant Reformation, as well as the patronizing attitude which implies that, even though Catholics have the "full truth," they should accept Protestants who have at least part of the truth. Catholic students need to realize that the Protestant tradition preserved a vital element in Christianity—the importance of a continual reform of the Church. I would suggest that the words of Protestant theologian George Lindbeck have value for Protestants and Catholics alike:

My own personal conclusion is that, in the contemporary eschatological-historical framework of thought, it is becoming increas-

59

ingly difficult to develop a comprehensive and consistent theological justification for either Protestantism or Roman Catholicism as they now exist. Even within history, quite apart from the reconciliation which we hope for at the end of time, and not only for the sake of the united Christian witness which is our theological work, we are compelled to long and pray for a church which is both Catholic and Reformed, and lacks the doctrinal presumptuousness in which both parties are now involved.[2]

Finally, teachers should try to expose their students to the activities of the National Council of Churches and the World Council of Churches. But they should also attempt to show them the differences between the major Protestant denominations such as Lutheranism, Episcopalianism and Methodism, pointing out the basic emphases in each group. Likewise teachers, even in a sympathetic presentation of Protestantism, must be careful to avoid a stereotyped, static view of its member groups. Many of the current reforms in Protestantism follow very closely the lines of change we are now witnessing in the Catholic Church as a result of Vatican Council II.

EASTERN CHRISTIANS

There is little to report with respect to Eastern Christians, whether Orthodox or those in union with Rome. They go virtually unmentioned in the instructional materials under examination. This is most unfortunate and needs to be corrected in the future. Almost nothing is said in the materials about the split between the Eastern and Western church, while hundreds of pages are devoted to the Reformation. In some textbooks, the Reformation is described as the first real break in Christianity, ignoring the much earlier separation of Eastern and Western Christianity, whose issues are just as profound and important to understand as those of the Reformation controversy. Students need to be presented with a fuller understanding of the history which eventually led to this separation of the two major segments of Christianity.

Also to be stressed in the process of improving the portrait of the Eastern churches is their viewpoint on tradition and the nature of the Church and her authority as well as the unique liturgical rites found in these Churches. Vatican Council II in its *Decree on the Catholic Churches of the Eastern Rite*[3] expressed unequivocably the position and the rights of the Eastern communities within the Roman Catholic Church and re-established privileges and customs which had been abolished in the past. It further expressed the hope for a corporate reunion of the Eastern Orthodox churches with the Roman Church. The Council insisted that the traditions of the Eastern churches which differ from those of the West, rather than harming unity, enrich the spirituality of the Church.

There are six main Eastern Catholic rites: the Chaldean, Syrian, Maronite, Coptic, Armenian and Byzantine. Their membership in the United States numbers about one million. There are also substantial numbers of Eastern Orthodox Christians in this country. Hence it is important that students know something about their history and background.

One final note of caution for the teacher. The Eastern Orthodox should never be simply classified as Protestants. Though they hold membership in the World Council of Churches, they consider themselves independent from the Protestant tradition. Their origins are due to an entirely different set of historical circumstances and their spirit differs significantly from Protestantism in many important ways.

NON-CHRISTIAN GROUPS

The positive portrait of non-Christian religious groups presented in the social studies materials was limited to pagans, Muslims and other Oriental religions, together with references to Buddha, Confucius and Laotze. The majority of the entries scored in this category referred to Mohammed and the brilliant Muslim culture. Positive references to pagans were not too numerous, but the few tabulated showed an acknowledgment of the positive qualities of some pagans. In one manual the teacher was advised to stress "a pagan ruler's respect for the dignity of man." Several publications acknowledged that pagans lead morally good lives.

History materials tended to focus on Islam. The positive portrait drawn by the authors stressed the religious spirit and patriotism of the Muslims, the great appeal of their religion, the sincerity of their members, and their religious practices of prayer, almsgiving, hospitality, and loyalty. Two examples:

Among the more important reasons for the remarkable expansion of Mohammedans were the strong patriotism and religious spirit inspired by that religion.

Moslems worship the God of Adam and Eve, of Moses and Abraham. . . . The Moslems are often very sincere in their love of God. They are not ashamed to mention his name respectfully in conversation, or to kneel at the hours of prayer in public places. They give alms to the poor, are hospitable to strangers and loyal to friends.

Most of the entries scored for the Muslim religious group concerned its flourishing medieval culture. These entries stressed that the Muslims accepted and further developed the best in the cultures they contacted or conquered. Emphasis was placed upon their excellent history, their great literary contributions in the realm of poetry and prose, and their scientific and philosophical works.

The Mohammedans, especially those in Spain, added some very important things to the civilization of Western Europe. Many of their beautiful mosques . . . and other buildings are still standing. Many of the Arabs were poets. Others wrote prose. Some were historians. The Arabs were great astronomers and also studied medicine.

A list of some of the words that have come into the English language from the Arabic as a result of their brilliant Moslem culture will illustrate the vastness and variety of their achievements.

In the liberal arts the Moslems were serious students of the Greek philosophers, especially Aristotle. Their translations of Aristotle and their commentaries on his works were introduced to the

Christian West in the twelfth century and made possible the work of the greatest of all Catholic philosophers, St. Thomas Aquinas.

Other references to non-Christians in the materials described the simplicity, zeal, and special virtues of the Oriental religions.

It appears that he [Buddha] was a remarkable man of zeal and mildness who led a life as simple as that of many Christian saints.

Many Chinese practice the teachings of Confucius. Confucius was a wise man who lived long ago. He taught the Chinese to honor their parents, to be gentle and polite, and to be honest and hard-working.

In other social studies textbooks the authors attacked directly suspected stereotypes of students and made them aware of the tragic aspects of the Crusades with regard to non-Christian groups. For example:

Contrary to the popular notion, the Arabs only occasionally spread their religion by the sword. Generally they were very tolerant, especially toward Christians and Jews whom they carefully distinguished from the heathen.

Unhappily they [the members of the First Crusade] had no mercy on the Moslem inhabitants, whom they slaughtered by the thousands.

The social studies units also contained some negative materials with respect to non-Christian groups. Most of it had to do with the supposed warlike spirit of Islam. Other references presented non-Christian ideals as essentially opposed to Christian ideals and described non-Christian religions as "gloomy."

Non-Christian ideals: contempt for those who are not as well off as we are; hatred of our enemies; refusal to accept God's will; indifference to religion and religious duties; selfish interest in our own welfare; take and use for our own benefit as much of the world's wealth as we can get; indifference to the needs of others; all-consuming desire to possess the things of this world; non-regard for family ties and affection.

The first religion in India of which anything is known was Hinduism; it was a gloomy religion with little hope for a brighter life after death.

The word Islam means obedience to God. Mohammed believed in the unity of God. "God is God and Mohammed is his prophet" was his slogan. Prayer, fasting, alms, and pilgrimages to Mecca were some of the Mohammedan ways of serving God. They did not preach this new religion but urged war on unbelievers.

The religion materials, by comparison, contained very little of significance with regard to the non-Christian groups. They concentrated heavily on Protestantism and Judaism, generally bringing in references to other religious outgroups only in the context of broad generalizations about the need for openness toward all religious peoples of the world.

As a result, much improvement still is required in the portrayal of non-Christian religions. Their presentation in Catholic materials has not been updated to the same extent as the Protestant portrait.

Catholics should begin to explore sympathetically the great religious traditions represented by Hinduism, Buddhism, and Islam. Protestant theologian Paul Tillich has seen the encounter of the Church with world religions as the *great* task for the future.[4] As Catholic students move into the age of the global village, a knowledge of the world's great religions will be essential for true harmony and creative peace among nations. This does not mean an abandonment of the Christian religious tradition, but a breaking out of an exclusive particularity. Tillich insists:

Christianity will be a bearer of the religious answer as long as it breaks through its own particularity. The way to achieve this is not to relinquish one's religious tradition for the sake of a universal concept which would be nothing but a concept. The way is to penetrate into the depth of one's own religion in devotion, thought and action. In the depth of every living religion there is a point at which the religion loses its importance, and that to which it points breaks through its particularity, elevating it to spiritual freedom and with it to a vision of the spiritual presence in other expressions of the ultimate meaning of man's existence. This is what Christianity must see in the present encounter of world religions.[5]

There is still far from sufficient appreciation of this spirit in Catholic teaching. When non-Christian religions are presented, the presentation frequently seems to make their religious convictions distant from and foreign to the Christian way of life. A much more thorough and sympathetic approach is needed that would help the student draw upon the insights of these religions as well as understand them. This has been urged upon Catholics by the *Declaration on the Relationship of the Church to Non-Christian Religions* issued by Vatican Council II.[6] In this document the Council fathers stressed that all people compose a single community, and have a single origin, since God made the whole race of men dwell over the entire face of the earth (cf. Acts 17:26). The peoples belonging to non-Christian religions have found answers to many of the profound mysteries of the human condition which deeply stir the human heart even today. The document goes on to praise the meditation and ascetic spirit of Hinduism, Buddhism's understanding of the radical insufficiency of the world, and Islam's worship of God through prayer, almsgiving and fasting. The Declaration sums up its attitude toward non-Christians with the following exhortation for Catholics:

Prudently and lovingly, through dialogue and collaboration with the followers of other religions, and in witness of Christian faith and life, acknowledge, preserve, and promote the spiritual and moral goods found among these men, as well as the values in their society and culture.[7]

In portraying the non-Christian religions, teachers should guard against the same type of stereotyping and static depiction mentioned in connection with Protestantism. Many of the Eastern religions are also experiencing changes and modifications in their life styles as the societies of which they are a part undergo modernization.

Finally, in some cases teachers may not even be aware that prejudicial expressions are in fact being used by them. Professor

Abdu-r-Rabb of Pakistan makes this point with reference to Islam in a paper presented to the 1968 International Conference of Christians and Jews.[8] Often, he says, ordinary Christians do not even know the correct name of Islam nor what to call its followers, who constitute approximately one-seventh of the world's population. Christians generally call the religion Mohammedism and its adherents Mohammedans. (Several excerpts from the social studies materials provide examples.) This designation offends Muslims because it implies that Islam is the product of the mind of Muhammad. Muslims believe that Islam is the right guidance given by God to mankind through his messenger, the prophet Mohammed. God revealed the same kind of guidance through Moses, Jesus and many others before Muhammad. The term Islam literally means "surrender." It is surrendering to God in order to obtain from him guidance in the right path.

Professor Abdu-r-Rabb also expressed regret over the subtle and sometimes not so subtle attempts he and other Muslims have encountered in North America to convert them, the portrayal of Muslims on television as dishonest and sexually perverted, and the failure of the Westerner to understand his name as a unit ("the servant of the Lord") which cannot be broken down into first name and surname in the Western fashion. This last situation is symptomatic of an attitude shared by many American Christians who think theirs is the only civilization, the only right way of life and the only criterion for judging right and wrong. "They do not consider," he says, "for a moment that they constitute only a small segment of the entire human race."[9]

What is to be concluded from the fact that the religion textbooks revealed the highest proportion of hostile and prejudiced comments regarding non-Catholic religious groups? Does it mean that the civil tradition of American democracy, so frequently invoked by the social studies units, provides a stronger foundation for positive attitudes than doctrinal assertions about the unity of mankind under the fatherhood of God? Does it imply that the task of inculcating the faith—more directly the responsibility of religion units than of social studies or literature, although, of course, the latter are profoundly related to the goals of a total

Catholic education—necessarily results in negative attitudes regarding other faiths? Or are there theological resources within Christianity, and specifically within Roman Catholicism, which can be better utilized to enlarge our sympathy and appreciation for other faiths with no loss of commitment and devotion to our own?

The noted scholar of ecumenism, Gregory Baum, O.S.A., has provided an exemplary analysis of how religion is both a source of prejudice and a force for its healing.[10] He points out that the Christian religion creates community, a close fellowship of the faithful, in which the means of salvation are available to them. Celebration of the sacraments renders it a sacred society, different from the worldly societies to which its members also belong. The belief that there was no salvation outside the Church led to the erection of a clearly visible dividing line—a "wall of truth"—between Christians and non-Christians.

For the Church's well-being, this wall had to be strong. It protected the ordinary Christian. Since salvation was limited to those inside, the wall intensified the Christian's appreciation of the importance of belonging to the Church. Christians would cross the wall and mingle with the men who lived beyond it only for the purpose of making converts. The converts were usually severed from their former associates and integrated into the Christian society. Missionary activity preserved and even strengthened the wall of truth that surrounded the Church.

Thus the Christian religion divided mankind into "we" and "they." This radical distinction influenced the way Christians interpreted their life in society, their personal associations and their political ideals. It served as the key for an understanding of history. We hold the truth; they are in error. We have access to salvation; they sit in darkness and are filled with fear. We are virtuous, understanding, liberated, cultured; they are treacherous, fanatical, superstitious, uncivilized. This deep division between "we" and "they" inevitably generated a sense of superiority. We are superior; they are inferior.

Dr. Thomas Szasz has analyzed the rhetoric of exclusion used by a we-group to affirm its own superiority and to exclude the others from their share in the goods of humanity.[11] The rhetoric of exclusion finds rational arguments or theological reasons to justify this self-elevation and make it acceptable even to men possessing a sensitive conscience. The rhetoric of exclusion which is manipulated by the leaders of society and endorsed and amplified by the members tries to assign an ever lower place to outsiders. They come to be regarded as inferior from every point of view. If this rhetoric goes on without restraint, the outsiders are eventually looked upon as less than human and their suppression becomes a moral ideal. In the end society will even approve of their extermination. They are no longer human and hence have forfeited the right to live. Such rhetoric of exclusion is far from uncommon in Christian literature. In many cases it has led to disastrous political and social consequences. History tells us of holy wars and the killing of infidels. It is this rhetoric of exclusion that has made Christianity a source of prejudice. Even today when the cruder forms of this exclusion have vanished, the rhetoric tends to remain with us and to perpetuate the inherited prejudices.

This is one pathological trend in religion. Fr. Baum points to a second. Christianity proposes a high moral ideal to men. It advocates holiness of life. The Christian claims to be free of the bonds of sin. He has become a servant of justice. His community is the holy Church. It is this high ideal of holiness that forces the Christian community to live up to its image of holy Church. Christians must present themselves as the holy fellowship of true believers, without division or conflict. Christian teaching creates an image to which the Church tends to cling at all costs. Often this image hinders the Church's self-understanding. The high ideal stops Christians from looking at who they really are.

This tendency appears in every society. But the higher the moral ideal, the more threatened a society is by the knowledge of the truth and the more vulnerable it becomes to paranoidal behavior. To escape facing up to the evil trends existing within it, a society will try to project them on outgroups. The outsiders become the embodiment of unfaithfulness, superstition, hostility and fanaticism. Christians see in others what they do not want to admit about themselves. Prejudice against others becomes a powerful defense against self-knowledge. The more "orthodox" and "holy" a religious community wants to become, the greater the potential for paranoidal behavior and the creation of prejudice.

These two pathological tendencies make religion a source of prejudice. But Fr. Baum sees in the Christian Gospel a power that heals men from prejudice, not only from that generated by their religion but from all prejudice created by human society as a whole.

The Christian Gospel does not divide mankind into two clearly defined groups of Christians and non-Christians. The Gospel does not define a radical distinction between "we" and "they." There is certainly a difference between Christians and those who do not regard themselves as followers of Christ. Yet according to Christ's teaching, the wonderful things God operates in Christians also are to be found among men who do not belong to the Church. We learn, moreover, that the opposition to good and the deafness to God's voice are attitudes also present within the Church. "Not everyone who says to me, 'Lord, Lord,' but he who does the will of my heavenly Father, shall enter the kingdom of heaven" (Mt. 7:21). According to the teaching of Christ men are judged not by their creed, but according to the attitude they show toward their neighbor in which their credal affirmations of faith, hope and love find visible embodiment. "Truly I say to you, as you did it to one of the least of these my brothers, you did it to me" (Mt. 25:40).

This line of thought has been greatly stressed in the present age. We have become more conscious of the universality of divine grace. There has developed among Christians a new awareness of the bonds uniting them to others. The brotherhood which is the work of God's grace extends beyond the Church to all men. The absolute loyalty of Christians is to the mystery of divine redemption that is revealed in Jesus Christ. This is doing the will of the Father; it is obeying the Spirit at work in the whole human family. This loyalty transcends the sociological reality of the Church. A Christian identifies himself with the institutional Church only conditionally; his loyalty is conditioned by the Gospel. His mission to serve the kingdom, to seek justice and resist evil, may

69

bring him into situations in which he must side with men of other religions or no religion against men of his own Church.

Because the loyalty of a Christian to any institution is conditioned by the Gospel, he is never willing to divide the human family into "we" and "they." The Gospel, moreover, rejects the radical distinction between "the holy" and "the unholy." In the teachings of Jesus the division between just men and sinners is undercut. According to the Gospel, sin had found its way into the lives of all men. To think of oneself as just and hence not needing redemption is an attitude contrary to Christian faith. To regard ourselves as just or the Church as just is to introduce a division into mankind that generates illness. The man who calls himself just and refers to others as sinners prevents himself from coming to self-knowledge. The "just" man is unprotected against his own destructive drives, for he never sees them. He will do harm to other people without knowing it.

The Gospel calls all men to conversion. It repeatedly summons the Christian to the acknowledgment of his destructiveness and the readiness to turn away from these layers of his personality to the new life that is being offered him. He is summoned to acknowledge his prejudices and use them to discover the evil inclinations in himself which he tries to hide. This call to conversion, therefore, is the remedy from the paranoia which threatens men. We are called to admit who we truly are, not before a judge but a Savior.

Hence the Gospel can free men from the prejudices created by their Christian as well as their national and cultural heritage. The Gospel warns men not to attach themselves to their own self-image. Conversion remains a permanent dimension of human life. As men learn to look at themselves as they are, they also come to acknowledge others as they are—their great qualities and their openness to the Spirit, as well as their smallness and their tendency to be closed. Such an understanding of the Gospel enables men to see reality as it is. Thus the two pathological trends which make the Christian religion a source of prejudice against others are counterbalanced and sometimes overcome through a sensitivity to the Gospel message which seeks to prevent men from dividing the world into "we" and "they" and "the holy" and the "unholy."

The question arises whether a community of people can survive without a wall around them and an appropriate rhetoric of exclusion. Will such a community inevitably dissolve into a wider cultural group? Is some prejudice required for the perpetuation of a religious society? Is it possible to retain one's particularity if one wholeheartedly endorses the universality of grace?

Universality, writes Fr. Baum, does not automatically imply an undifferentiated human community. It does not envisage the removal of all distinctions. It is not by becoming less faithful to one's religious tradition that a man loses his prejudices and experiences fellowship with others. On the contrary, it is by becoming more Christian, by experiencing the unity of the Christian community and his membership in a particular people, that a man is able to acknowledge other people for what they are and willing to embrace them as brothers, without wishing to destroy their heritage and draw them into an undifferentiated religious melting pot. Only if particularity and universality are not looked upon as opposites can there be any hope of eliminating prejudice.

We are currently experiencing a breakdown of closed societies. People are reluctant to commit themselves uncritically to any institution or any system. Men in our day want to embrace with love the community to which they belong and the institutions which serve it, but they also want to learn and to grow, and to participate in various ways in the human community beyond the one to which they are primarily committed. Men refuse to solve their problems by seeking logical consistency with a full-blown system or by invoking unquestioning loyalty to an institution. If they have deep convictions, they still remain open to the new, willing to test reality and to change their viewpoints and policies if need be. This we see taking place in the churches, in the political world and even in communist societies.

In our time people are unwilling to belong to a single society in a total and exclusive way. They reject a nationalism which identifies cultural, political, economic, linguistic and religious values with a single society. People want to love their own and be loyal to them. But according to various levels of identification they also desire to be part of other communities.

A similar development can be observed in religious societies. A Catholic wants to be a loyal member of his Church, but he does not want to belong to his Church in a way that would prevent him from sharing community with Protestants. In some way he also wants to belong to them, to bear the burden with them and rejoice with them. Catholics want to participate with Jews and with people everywhere who are concerned with service and reconciliation. Today many Christians would shrink from belonging to any community so exclusively that they would cease to be open to various forms of communication with others. Today multiple loyalties do not normally divide; they intensify our self-possession, they make us more ourselves, they give us greater strength to engage in the ministry of reconciliation and peace.

Moreover, writes Fr. Baum, only an "open" religious community can survive in the future. In the static society characteristic of the past, roots were necessary for men to find their self-identity. We belonged to a town or a village, to a certain country, to a religion. We knew who we were; we could locate ourselves in the psychological sense, through our roots. If we were cut off from these roots, we began to drift, looking in vain for strength and conviction and eventually threatened by isolation and depression. Today many of these static patterns have gone by the boards. We move easily from one place to another. We belong to several communities, we may have lived in several countries, we may have friends and colleagues all over the world. We often identify with movements and causes not only in our own country but abroad.

In contemporary society we are unable to attain self-possession by seeking the kind of roots that were available to people in the past. If we look for roots in a single community, we will be uncertain of ourselves all of our lives. To have a sense of belonging in our day, we must participate in several communities on different levels.

If it is true that modern man cannot find his roots in the stable society of the past and that he seeks his friends in a variety of contexts, in shifting alliances tuned to changing situations, where is his vital center? What prevents schizophrenia? For Fr. Baum, the unity of the personality is created by the person's orientation toward growth and unity which, according to Christian faith, is the redemptive work of God in the heart of man. Man is united by the mystery of grace that is present in him and which, as a Christian, he acknowledges in Jesus Christ. The roots of men are not from below, they are from above. The self-possession of man and his freedom from prejudice are provided by the multiple participation in several communities, a participation maintained in a living and creative unity by the presence of God to human life.

Obviously, Fr. Baum's analysis is not a simple formula for the instant cure of prejudice, but it suggests certain approaches that can help Christian teachers become aware of and overcome shortcomings in the textual materials they use. One is a wholehearted acceptance of the ethnic and religious diversity of the world, an ability to see that richness and variety as a positive good, not as a threat to faith. For another, we must resist the temptation to divide the world into the holy and the unholy, the saved and the sinners. We must realize that the "we's" and "they's" we encounter are not permanent and unyielding categories, that according to principle we will sometimes side with our own against others and sometimes side with others against our own.

FOOTNOTES

1. William Clancy, Gustave Weigel, and Thomas O'Dea, "Protestant-Catholic Dialog.," *Catholic Mind,* September-October, 1959, pp. 399-401. Quoted in Sister Rose Thering, *op. cit.,* p. 264.
2. George Lindbeck, "The Framework of Catholic-Protestant Disagreement," in T. Patrick Burke (ed.), *The Word in History,* New York: Sheed & Ward, pp. 102-119.
3. Cf. Walter M. Abbott, S.J. (ed.), *The Documents of Vatican II,* New York: America Press, 1966.
4. *Christianity and the Encounter of the World Religions.* New York: Columbia University Press, 1963. Also cf. *The Future of Religions.* Evanston: Harper & Row, 1966.
5. *Christianity and the Encounter of the World Religions,* p. 97.

6. Cf. Walter M. Abbott, S.J., *op. cit.*, p. 660.
7. *Ibid.*, pp. 662-663.
8. "The Christian Image of Islam," paper presented to 1968 International Conference of Christians and Jews, York University, Toronto, Canada.
9. *Ibid.*, p. 3.
10. Cf. "Religion and Prejudice," paper delivered at the 1968 International Conference of Christians and Jews, York University, Toronto, Canada.
11. Quoted by Gregory Baum in *The Ecumenist,* March/April, 1968, p. 134.

CHAPTER 5

FINDINGS REGARDING JUDAISM

The findings of the St. Louis study as they bear on Jews and Judaism will be reported in this chapter, and some of the implications of these findings for Christian education and Christian self-understanding will be explored in the following chapters.

If this seems an inordinate attention to Jewish content in a book dealing with intergroup relations in Catholic education, it is because problems related to attitudes toward Jews and Judaism run deeper, and are more central to the Christian self-image, than for any other group. The few instances of prejudice against racial or ethnic groups encountered in the textbook studies seem peripheral, requiring relatively simple correction, mainly the addition of supplementary information. Prejudice against non-Catholic religious groups, while it presents a somewhat greater problem, still seems correctible without any serious dislocation of traditional Catholic self-understanding. Indeed, some of the abuses—many of the distorted references to Protestants, for example—have simply fallen by the wayside with the growth of ecumenical consciousness and the general educational shift from an apologetical to a kerygmatic approach.*

But Christianity is so inextricably involved with Judaism, both theologically and historically, and the way Catholicism views Judaism is so profoundly related to its corporate self-image, that some treatment in depth of the historical and theological encounter with Judaism is required.

There is very little to report from the literature study with regard to Judaism. Sister Gleason did not designate the Jewish group as a separate category but merely relied on a general non-Christian category for purposes of tabulation. But the vast majority of visibility scores for the non-Christian group in the four sets she analyzed stood below 3 percent. Hence it is obvious that students were exposed to virtually no characters clearly identifiable as Jews. Whether this is due to the compilers or simply reflects the literary scene from which the compilers had to select material is open to question.

The social studies findings revealed only a minimal presence of materials dealing with Judaism. Jewish exposure ranked lowest among the seven ethnic-racial groups. What materials there were proved to be generally favorable in their presentation of the Jewish people. Yet scores for the Jewish group, as for the other religious groups in the social studies materials, stood considerably below those achieved by the racial-ethnic groups.

References to Judaism in social studies units pertained primarily to Jews of the ancient period, though there were occasional allusions to manifestations of the Jewish spirit in subsequent periods up to our time. The positive portrait of ancient Jews laid emphasis on the special mission of the Jews, and their contribution of monotheism to the world was depicted as perhaps their greatest contribution of all. The Jews are called "a great nation" and the "chosen people" by the textbook writers and are pictured as courageous and faithful in the fulfillment of their special mission. For example:

The Hebrews did not build a great empire. They did not give us a

*Sister Thering found that textbooks employing a kerygmatic, liturgical or historical approach tended to score more positively than materials using an apologetical approach.

calendar as the Egyptians and Babylonians did. They did not give us coins as the Lydians did. They did not give us an alphabet as the Phoenicians did. But the Hebrews gave us something more valuable than any of these things. They kept alive the belief in the one true God. They were also the people from whom the redeemer was born.

Catholics have a special obligation to be charitable toward the Jews because the Jewish religion was the forerunner of the Catholic Church. . . . Then, too, our Lord, our Lady, St. Joseph, and the early disciples and apostles were all Jews.

The Hebrews . . . preserved the belief in the one true God . . . [and] gave us the Bible as a religious book and as great literature.

Some of the social studies references stress the fact that although the Jews constituted only a very small segment of the population of the ancient world, they did much for civilization past and present, for "human learning," out of all proportion to their numbers:

The ancient peoples made outstanding contributions to human living and civilization. . . . The Jews, despite the smallness of their number, preserved for us the knowledge of the supernatural destiny which God intended for all mankind.

This chapter serves as a good place to emphasize the importance of the Hebrews in the story of Christianity and the value of the Bible as a source of history, a work of literature, and a religious document. . . . From this study [of the Bible and history] the students may gain a better appreciation of the many contributions of the ancient Hebrews to modern culture and also a background for the modern problem of Palestine.

Jews were praised in several publications as having cultural traits that should be imitated by Christians:

The Jewish people have many culture traits which are definitely to be imitated by Christians, for example, their regard for family harmony, and their care for the aged and poor.

Other references tabulated as positive called the students' attention to the important role of Jewish people in American life, their talents and achievements in the professions and in industry, and their devotion to duty and hard work:

Many immigrants have suffered discrimination due to prejudices against them not because of their national origin, but because of their religion. . . . For Jews the discrimination has probably been intensified because of their numbers in certain cities and because they are an exceptionally gifted and hard-working group, for there are more Jewish leaders in the professions, industry, finance and commerce than might be expected of their total numbers.

A resident of Philadelphia, this colonist of Jewish faith [Haym Salomon] raised three quarters of a million dollars for the colonial cause to help America win freedom.

On occasion the social studies materials also contained brief mention of the cooperative work of Catholics, Protestants and Jews on basic social problems facing American society in our time. Especially singled out for their work were the National Conference of Christians and Jews and the American Jewish Committee.

Several references spoke of the sufferings of Jews during the Nazi period and underscored the evil of any forms of prejudice toward Jews in our own day:

The Jews, so the Nazis professed to believe, were mortal enemies of Germany and all other nations. This was a fantastically untrue belief; yet it proved a powerful political force because people, when they are suffering, easily become credulous and are on the lookout for a scapegoat.

Because a number of Catholics in the United States are anti-Jewish, it is important to stress Catholic truth in this course. Sociologists need to have the facts clear; in religion classes, the topic takes on added significance.

For example, many Catholics have irrational emotions about Jews. . . . They would not have these prejudices if they reflected upon what they were doing. Not only is it un-Christian to have prejudices, but to have prejudices which lead to discrimination against groups is also un-American.

Very few negative references were recorded for the Jewish group. The following represent the general tone of the few that were discovered in the materials by Sister Mudd:

They [Jews] are the world's saddest people because they turned away from Jesus.

For the Jews the basis of justice was "an eye for an eye"; their attitude was one of hatred for all non-Jews, whom they lumped together as Gentiles; and they were strict isolationists from all non-believers.

Although the Jewish people rejected the redeemer when he came into their midst, the divine plan of God was definitely accomplished.

After the rejection of Christ and his crucifixion by the Jews, their holy city was destroyed in 70 A.D.

When the Jews refused to accept Jesus he let their enemies overcome them.

To characterize the Jewish portrait in the social studies materials, it is helpful to distinguish between ancient and modern settings. In the setting of ancient (pre-Christian and early Christian) times, both the positive and negative references to Jews closely parallel the kinds of statements found in the religion textbooks. That is, the negative references center around the Jewish rejection of Christianity. (It is worth noting that these were the only *kinds* of negative references to Jews in the social studies units.) The positive references generally center around religious contributions such as monotheism and the Bible, or the Jewish background of Jesus, his family and early followers. Whether these "positive" statements are positive for Judaism, or positive only for those aspects of Judaism which became incorporated into Christianity, is an interesting question treated more fully below.

In a more modern setting—that is, when Jews are discussed as an immigrant group in the United States, or as a people who have suffered from discrimination and bigotry—the references are sympathetic and there is no evidence of prejudice. There is, however, the familiar problem of silence. The textbooks said nothing about the development of contemporary Judaism. Except for a few references to the Nazi holocaust, little is done to indicate the magnitude of that crime, which resulted in the destruction of half of European Jewry. Nothing at all is included about the development of Zionism and the modern state of Israel. Omission of this subject may very well be the result of the previously-mentioned preoccupation with native and Western European history. Still, given the centrality of Israel to Jewish existence and the importance of the Middle East in world affairs today, it is curious to find that Israel—when it is referred to at all—still tends to be designated "Palestine."

It is in the religion textbooks that the special problems Catholics face in writing about Jews and Judaism emerge most clearly. While Jews are almost unrepresented in the literature materials and are the least visible group in the social studies units, they are the most visible group in the religion materials for all publishers without exception. This is hardly an unexpected finding, since it is virtually impossible to teach Christianity—particularly such aspects as revelation, the life of Jesus and the origins of the early Church—without significant reference to Jews and Judaism.

What are the sources of positive and negative references to Jews in the religion textbooks? The representative excerpts provided by Sister Thering indicate that the bulk of the positive and neutral references are associated with the Jewish heritage of Christianity. For example:

Jews and Gentiles, representing the whole human race, have paid their homage to the child Jesus.

Abraham, father of the people of God, yesterday and today.

Catholics of the world regardless of their nationality are all spiritually Semites. We are all children of Israel. God's revelation of himself to the patriarchs and his promise of good things handed on to the children of Israel reach down through time to us who believe, trust in, and love the one true God and who enjoy good and wonderful things beyond compare as his adopted children and the mystical body of his divine Son Jesus Christ.

Christ first revealed his presence on earth to the Jews, the chosen people of the Old Testament, and indeed, to the humblest and poorest and most believing among the Jews, the shepherds.

News of the birth of Jesus Christ, the Son of God, had been brought to the Jews by angels. The Jews, however, formed only a small part of the whole human race living on earth at that time. Gentiles, or non-Jews, were to be saved by Jesus as well as Jews.

While all the above were scored as positive for Jews, it is clearly implied that the Judaism which is praised culminated in Christianity; the Jews who are esteemed are praised for their implied acceptance of Christianity. While the textbooks acknowledge the spiritual wealth of Judaism, they infer that these riches were totally absorbed by Christianity. Judaism's value as a religion appears to be exhausted in its contribution to the Christian heritage.

This raises profound questions involving Christianity's self-definition. Christianity has been described from its beginnings as the fulfillment of Judaism. It was the *new* Israel with a *new* covenant. It was founded by the *new* Moses and followed the *New* Testament. All of these "news" have traditionally left little room for any serious understanding of the continuation of Judaism, of "old" Israel, as a dynamic, growing religion and culture, as relevant to the modern world as it was to people of ancient times.

The overwhelming majority of negative references concerning Jews were concentrated around the themes of: (1) the Jewish rejection of Christianity and the consequent divine curse inflicted on this people; (2) the Jewish role in the crucifixion; and (3) comments regarding the Pharisees. For example, in the first category:

In spite of the countless graces given to the chosen people, they voluntarily blinded themselves to Christ's teaching.

Christ replied to the question in the mind of his listeners as to what the owner of the vineyard will do to these wicked vine dress-

81

ers. He will destroy them. He will turn over the vineyard to others who will render him fruits. His prophecy was partially fulfilled in the destruction of Jerusalem and more fully in the rejection by God of the chosen people.

Christ then returned to his teaching on humility by telling them the parable of the great supper and of the guests who refused to come. This is one of those parables which refers to the obstinacy of the Jews in spurning the Gospel.

Christ, by his miracles and preaching, tried to conquer the obstinacy of the Jews and to bring them to repentance. The Jews, on the contrary, by the bad influence of their hypocrisy and pride, hindered the spread of the knowledge of God among other nations.

The Jews as a nation refused to accept Christ, and since his time they have been wanderers on the earth without a temple, or a sacrifice, and without the Messiah.

The same culpable blindness which closed the eyes of the Jewish leaders to the Scriptures, which portrayed the Messiah as a suffering redeemer and not as a military conqueror, also closed their eyes to Christ's resurrection and its significance.

In his study of Protestant curriculum materials, Dr. Bernhard Olson notes that the question of responsibility for the crucifixion has historical, psychological and theological dimensions. In Protestant lessons, he observes:

. . . the guilt for Golgotha is either particularized or universalized, i.e., the meaning of the event is applied either to particular groups or to all groups. . . . For some, the crucifixion stands as their call to martyrdom. For others, who particularize it, it signifies the rejection of the Jews and their abandonment to fate. To those who universalize it, it points to the disobedience of all mankind (symbolized by Jew and Gentile together) and to the divine mercy conferred upon all humanity.[1]

The same observation may be applied to Catholic lessons as well. When the theological significance of the crucifixion is universalized, all mankind is seen to be involved. Statements of this kind were not infrequent in the religion materials. For example:

Why did Christ suffer death? . . . As Christ's powers were infinite, he could have redeemed the sins of a thousand worlds by shedding one drop of his blood; but he chose of his own free will to suffer such excruciating torments in order to show his love for us and to make us realize the enormity of sin.

Did Christ suffer for all men or only for those who will be saved? Christ died for each and every person who ever lived or shall live.

Why Christ suffered. That *all* men might be united in love and peace with one another, and that all men might be united in love with God; it was for this that Christ prayed and it was for this that Christ suffered and died.

The difficulty, however, was that this universal viewpoint was seldom brought to bear in discussions of the specific events which led up to the crucifixion. Thus, the Catholic student may be informed that the "sins of all men" were responsible for Christ's suffering, but this theological interpretation will remain an abstraction if it is not meaningfully applied to concrete descriptions of the event. In the representative excerpts from the religion materials, it is *Jewish* culpability for the suffering and death of Christ that is stressed, rather than the sins of all mankind. The term "the Jews" is frequently used to denote the enemies of Jesus without the corrective information that a limited number of individuals, and not the entire Jewish population of Palestine, is in question. This terminology heightens the impression of unique and collective Jewish guilt:

However, when the mob saw this, the chief priests took up a cry that put a curse on themselves and on the Jews for all time: "His blood be upon us and our children."

There can be no doubt that the Jews did everything they could to discredit the story [of the resurrection]. But the best story they could invent was that the disciples had stolen the body of Jesus from the tomb.

The worst deed of the Jewish people [was] the murder of the Messiah.

The Jews wanted to disgrace Christ by having him die on the cross.

Since Pilate could not find anything wrong with Christ, he decided to disfigure his pure and beautiful body, so that even the bloodthirsty Jews would back down and say that Christ had had enough.

The third negative theme in the materials concerned with Judaism was in many ways the worst of all. Passages referring to the Pharisees were among the most negative encountered in the textbooks. One basic series depicted the Pharisees in such a distorted fashion that the student would find it virtually impossible to sense any human identification with them or to believe that they acted out of human motivation:

No man is less pitied than one who has deliberately gouged out his own eyes. Hence, no one has sympathy for the Pharisees because they deliberately made themselves blind to the inspiring miracles and teachings of Christ. They were not ignorant men; if anything, they were experts in the Law. If anyone should have recognized the Messiah, they should have. The fact that they, of all people, didn't know Christ for what he was, is due to their jealousy and prejudice.

The Pharisees weren't much interested in seeing that God was honored on the Sabbath; they wanted their own laws observed.

They willfully refused to accept Christ as the Messiah, and they neglected the duty of brotherly love.

They were shocked to see racketeers selling sheep and doves in the building. . . . This was his first meeting with the "Temple Gang," that is, the scribes and Pharisees and priests who used religion to build up their own power among the people.

Some revealing insights about the manner in which the various textbooks examined by Sister Thering treated the same topics emerged from a contrast between some highly negative passages and more corrective and moderate selections. In the following examples, all of the "A" statements are taken from the particular textbook series which received the highest positive score for the Jewish group. Selections marked "B" appeared in several other series used in the study. While each set of comments treats of the same topics, it is clear that the "A" selections tend to be somewhat more corrective (though still generally inadequate) than the blatant distortions of the "B" group.

"A" SELECTIONS

We can, of course, hardly blame the crowds for not understanding our Lord's words, but he knew that they could not grasp his meaning. He even told them so. He said they were taking his words in too material, too "fleshly" a sense.

So it was that many Jews in our Lord's time were looking forward to the coming of a prophet who would introduce an age of true religion and of great closeness to Yahweh and who would bring even the Gentiles to worship the God of Israel. They seem to have called this awaited one simply the "prophet." Whether or not they thought he would be the same person as the Davidic Messiah we cannot be sure. Some of them may have done so. Most of them, however, seem to have forgotten that the ideal prophet in Isaiah (40—55) was a suffering prophet; they did not expect the awaited prophet to suffer.

To love one's enemy and to forgive injuries which one has received were lessons hard for the Jews to learn, as they are hard for all of us.

"B" SELECTIONS

The question of the Jews when Christ told them the secret, "How can this man give us His flesh to eat?" was a thoughtless one. Just because they could not understand, they would not believe.

The Jews rejected Christ mainly because they expected him to found a never-ending kingdom, as was foretold in the prophecies. This he really did, but the kingdom he founded—the Church— was a spiritual one, not a temporal one such as the carnal Jews were hoping for.

Why did the Jews commit the great sin of putting God himself to death? It was because our Lord told them the truth, because he preached a divine doctrine that displeased them, and because he told them to give up their wicked ways.

In the following chapters we will explore ways of confronting the problems involved in Jewish-Christian relations insofar as they pertain to the field of education with the hope of improving the portrait of Judaism that will be presented to future Catholic students.

FOOTNOTE

1. Olson, Faith and Prejudice, *op. cit.*, p. 206.

CHAPTER 6

CHRISTIAN EDUCATION
AND THE JEWISH PEOPLE

As previously noted, many Catholic teachers are presently in a dilemma about the proper attitude toward Judaism. They are sufficiently acquainted with the conciliar statement from Vatican Council II to realize that some of the textual presentations of Judaism described in previous chapters have resulted in gross injustice and suffering for Jews. Yet they are confused about what the new approach should emphasize, and how the new attitudes of the Church are to be reconciled with the apparent hostility to Jews in the New Testament.

This chapter will attempt to resolve some of the confusion. Not all questions can be answered at this time. Since many of the issues which affect the Jewish portrait in Catholic educational materials involve the Church's traditional self-understanding, their ultimate resolution must await considerable discussion by theologians and scholars. In the meantime, much can be done to correct the distortions found in Catholic textbooks, and to bring existing theological and scholarly resources to bear on the sensitive themes in ways that will be helpful to Catholic teachers.

NEW ATTITUDES TOWARD THE PHARISEES

Dr. Bernhard Olson, who directed the study of Protestant church school materials, has detailed ways in which the portrait of the Pharisees can be improved simply by a careful approach to the New Testament itself.[1] To begin with, the New Testament clearly does not present anything like a total condemnation of the Pharisees. Jesus conversed with a Pharisee and found him "not far from the kingdom of God." He was on sociable terms with several Pharisees and on occasion consented to be their guest. Some Pharisees came to his defense on certain occasions, and two Pharisees were responsible for giving Jesus a decent burial. The Pharisees are in no way implicated in the death of Jesus by any of the four Gospel writers.

Moreover, Dr. Olson writes, even if the Pharisees are seen to play a negative role, they are made more human by a theological perspective that shows them as representing all of humanity, including ourselves. In Jesus' entanglements with the Pharisees, he was speaking to all men. We should seek to identify ourselves with the Pharisees; Jesus stands in judgment on all of us. Thus the Pharisees cannot simply be relegated to the depths of sinful humanity. It is the very goodness of the Pharisees—for they were the best men of their day—which we must come to understand in order to grasp how even the best of men are subject to the demonic forces that influence every man, Pharisee or Christian.

Such an approach to the Pharisees will significantly affect a teacher's presentation of such scriptural passages as the twenty-third chapter of Matthew. Instead of degrading the Pharisees to such an extent that the Christian student has difficulty in seeing in them even an ounce of human sensitivity, the self-inclusion perspective leads to Christian self-criticism. Every point Jesus makes against the Pharisees, even the accusation of blindness to God's deeds, becomes a possible stricture against contemporary Christian life. The assumption is that to see what the Pharisees were doing is to see what it is we are doing and how Jesus' words can apply to us who have to face many of the same external pressures that were incumbent upon the Pharisees.

It is important therefore for Christian educators to realize that a perspective on the Gospels that pits man in opposition to Jesus results in an overall positive emphasis in the Jewish portrait as a whole. The Jew comes to be regarded as distinctively human, as a person similar in nature to the Christian student who is discussing him. Both are capable of much good as well as profound evil. The negative portrait of the Pharisees is utilized in combination with a positive expression for ingroup self-criticism and to achieve the goals of Christian education—self-knowledge, repentance and faith.

Even with this self-critical perspective, however, it would still be an injustice to the Christian student to limit his understanding of the Pharisees to the New Testament. For the primary intent of the Gospels was to describe the acts and words of Jesus in a way that the "Word of God" would be clearly manifest. Only those incidents and explanatory materials which contributed to an appreciation of Jesus' message and mission were preserved in the oral tradition. Everything else was left aside. The nature of the Pharisaic revolution in Judaism and the deepening of religious life it produced as well as the differences that existed within the Pharisaic schools[2] were clearly outside of the scope of the Gospel writers' interest. As a result, almost nothing is said about the positive relationship which existed between some Pharisees and Jesus. Only when Jesus' teachings are contrasted with some segment of Pharisaic interpretation and practice, especially when they stood in open conflict, are the Pharisees sketched in any detail. The Gospel writers make no attempt to provide non-Jews with a comprehensive description of the Pharisees. This would have been entirely beside the point.

We must therefore turn to extra-biblical sources for some appreciation of the multi-faceted nature of Judaism in the time of Jesus, and for an understanding of the development of Pharisaic Judaism. Such an understanding is vital to Christian students—not only because the widespread impression of a monolithic Judaism in the intertestamental and New Testament periods is inaccurate and unfair to Jews, but because this movement, which probably had its origins in the period of the Babylonian Exile and eventually came to be called Pharisaism, has profoundly influenced Christian thought. The teachings of Jesus and Paul are both deeply rooted in Pharisaic doctrines and practices.[3]

The Pharisees emphasized the worth of each individual person in the sight of God in a way not previously stressed in Judaism. Pharisaism opposed the primacy of the priestly, cultic system favored by the Sadducees. In its place the Pharisees substituted an emphasis on the direct relationship of each individual to God the Father. The system of Jewish law was transformed from a rigid legalism into a response to a sense of God's presence in the world and a means of salvation. Pharisaism internalized Jewish law and made it a matter of personal conscience. The individual could know where he stood in his relationship with God only by scrutinizing his individual deeds, for the *halakah*, "the way," had been made known to him and his veering from the path through sin could not be hidden from God. God, on the other hand, showed his concern for the individual as a person, never leaving him to himself.

The centrality of the individual in Pharisaic Judaism is nowhere more strikingly revealed than in a passage in the Mishnah* dealing with the admonishment of witnesses about to testify in a trial involving the death penalty:

You should be aware that judgments involving property are not the same as judgments involving life. In property matters an error in testimony can be atoned for through a money payment, but in a matter of life and death, his [the victim's] blood and the blood of his descendants depend upon it, to the end of time. . . . For this reason man was created one, to teach you that anyone who destroys a single human soul is reckoned by Scripture as having destroyed the entire world. And anyone who preserves a single soul, it is as though he kept the entire world alive.[4]

The dignity of the individual is further highlighted in another passage from the same section of the Mishnah:

The greatness of the Holy One, Blessed Be He, is attested by the

*The Mishnah is the record of the oral law (adhered to by the Pharisees, rejected by the Sadducees), taught and interpreted in the academies of Palestine from about the second pre-Christian century onward.

fact that whereas a human being in making coins from a single stamp can only impress upon them the same likeness, the king of kings, the Holy One, Blessed Be He, stamps every individual with the form of the first man, and each individual is different from every other. For this reason everyone is obligated [bound by law] to say, "It was on my account that the world was created!"[5]

The oral law interpretations of the Pharisaic rabbis reshaped the lofty injunctions of the great Jewish prophets and gave them a concrete order and structure. Every commonplace, daily human action could become sacred if it were seen, as the rabbis insisted it should be viewed, as an act of worship. The loving deed, the *mitzvah,* became more important than the Temple cult. Through the *mitzvah* approach a life-style was developed which could persist and grow long after the destruction of the Temple during the war with Rome in the first century A.D.

The Pharisaic rabbis developed a new system of rituals. One Jewish writer has called them "rituals of interpersonal behavior."[6] The commandments of the written Torah (the Pentateuch) contained very specific and detailed rules covering the offering of sacrifices and the duties of priests. But what precisely did the Torah mean when it said "Honor thy father and thy mother" or "Love thy neighbor as yourself" or "Remember that you were once slaves in the land of Egypt"? It was such questions that became the central focus of rabbinic teaching, and the answers made the oral law more than a mere commentary on the written law. The Pharisees deepened and humanized the older tradition. As the priests had centered their attention on codifying the cultic ritual, so the rabbis in a sense tried to codify love, loyalty, and human compassion. In so doing they hoped to make these inescapable religious duties incumbent upon every Jew. What the Pentateuch had stated as general propositions, the Pharisees spelled out as specific religious and moral duties. They effectively renewed Jewish religion by translating what had been only prophetic sentiment into a personal religion built upon "Propositions-in-action." Extending hospitality to the traveler, visiting the sick of all religious groups, giving charity anonymously, burying the dead, and helping to bring peace to those who lacked it: these duties were never clearly set forth in the Hebrew Bible although they were generally felt in spirit. The rabbis fashioned such duties into new commandments or *mitzvot,* which highlighted the role of prayer over sacrifice, and gave each person in Israel a priestly function.

Though each individual person was seen in Pharisaic theology as the world in microcosm, the rabbis had no desire to totally privatize religion or to establish the individual as the moral ultimate. Their development of the dignity of the individual within Judaism was set within the context of the traditional belief in the primacy of Israel the people. Without one of the two elements, person and community, the other lost much of its meaning in the Pharisaic perspective.

To guarantee the vitality of Israel as the people of God, as a holy nation and a kingdom of priests, the rabbis set up a system whereby the Hebrew Scriptures became the constitutional base for the corporate life of the Jewish community. But while the law continued to be regarded as of divine origin in the eyes of the rabbis, they added to it a dynamism and an expansive quality through their notion of the oral law. The biblical commandments were to be searched anew in a continuing effort to find new significance for the life of the community in its role as witness to the presence of God.

This major Pharisaic breakthrough in the approach to the Torah prevented the petrification of the Jewish religious spirit and paved the way for the periodic regeneration of Jewish religious attitudes and practices. The Pharisees won a theological victory over the Sadducees—priests who had been the rulers of the Jewish people. The rabbis never denied that the priests had been specially consecrated to administer the rituals of the Temple. But such consecration, the Pharisees argued, had given them no other religious authority even though the Sadducees claimed that the Pentateuch had been entrusted to the priests alone for interpretation. The Pharisees went back to Scriptural accounts of Sinai where Moses gave the Law to the whole people, not to any special group. According to the Pharisees the oral law was to be transmitted by the people from generation to generation. The rabbis took a fixed and unyielding tradition that had become glued to the hands of the priests and handed it over to the people as a whole. Those who studied and mastered the tradition were considered qualified to teach it, explain it, and ultimately even to amplify it. The rise of the Pharisees thus marked a radical moment in the history of Judaism and in the pre-history of Christianity which grew out of the Pharisaic spirit.

The Pharisees established adult academies for higher learning as popular institutions where lifelong study of the Torah could become an important communal preoccupation. In these creative circles brilliant students of the Torah debated their differing interpretations of the commandments. Many different schools vied with one another for a claim upon the people's allegiance. Their arguments, debates and conclusions have been preserved in what is called the Talmud, which exists in two versions, the Palestinian Talmud and the Babylonian Talmud. An important feature of the Talmud is the inclusion of all views, minority as well as majority. Even when the majority felt that the minority was clearly in error, the minority position was still recorded. This was more than simple respect for the power of human reason or intellectual honesty on the part of the rabbis. This attitude of openness formed the very cornerstone for future growth, maturation and renewal of the collective Jewish spirit. For if a minority group of Pharisees could reshape a tradition long locked in the dormant and authoritative arms of the priestly class, there might come a time in the future when yet another minority would need to be heard and followed. (In similar vein, dissenting opinions of our Supreme Court judges have become, on later occasions, the law of the land.) It was this special genius of rabbinic Judaism that molded and kept the Jews as one people throughout the world in spite of diverse and sometimes even contradictory interpretations of various groups and schools.

The rabbis taught that Israel had been called into existence for the sake of the Torah, but they made it quite clear that the Torah could live only through the people. By their emphasis on service to the world through membership in a distinctive people, the rabbis helped the community of Israel survive its national destruction at the hands of the Romans. They realized that if the Jewish people ceased to exist, the Torah would disappear from the face of the earth. Jewish spiritual life demanded a community to support, strengthen and enhance it. Because the Torah was a gift to the whole people, and since all shared equally in the responsibility to witness to it and hand it down to others, the collective life and destiny came to possess in Pharisaic Judaism a sacred calling and significance of its own. The whole people assumed in Pharisaic theology the role occupied by the Church in Christian thought. The whole people shared an irrevocable, divine vocation *as a people*. It is for this reason that Talmudic legislation extends far beyond the strictly theological frontiers to all aspects of corporate existence—social, economic and interpersonal.

The full "victory" of Pharisaism took place in the year 70 A.D. when Jerusalem fell to the Romans. The day of the Temple and the priesthood was over in Judaism. The rabbi now became the authoritative and unchallenged heir of both the prophetic and the priestly legacies. The synagogue likewise came into full prominence at this time as a radical religious center substituting prayer for sacrifice and making biblical study and interpretation into an act of worship.

Rabbinic Judaism did not consciously create the synagogue, but it did shape and adapt it as a vehicle of ethical universalism and its faith in the religious vocation of the Jewish people as the community of Israel. From its very inception the notion of the synagogue was rooted in the congregation rather than in a sacred place, a votive shrine, or a pretentious public building. Even when Jews returned to Palestine after the exile and constructed the second Temple, they retained a strong attachment to the synagogal form of religious expression. In spite of the presence of the new Temple, popular religious emphasis began to shift, even though only imperceptibly at first, from the sacramental office of the priests to the people themselves and from the holy place of worship to the worshipers. It was this spirit that no doubt motivated Jesus' attack on the money changers at the Temple. In the eyes of the Pharisees the whole people were the holy congregation, a theme that reappears in the first epistle of Peter.

The synagogal conception of the Pharisees appears in microcosmic form in what is called the *edah,* which the rabbis sanctioned as a formal religious congregation consisting of ten or more males. Wherever Jews assembled, whether in private homes, at the city gates or in the fields, they could form a congregation. More and more the *edah* notion came to dominate and invigorate Jewish thought. As a perennial reminder of the supreme sanctity of the Temple, the synagogue prayers were orientated toward Mount Zion in Jerusalem. The rabbis even specifically prayed for the rebuilding of the Temple. But, in effect, the synagogue transcended the Temple in the lives of the people because it became more than a "house of God." It was, more importantly, the "house of the people of God." The synagogue also took on functions outside of the realm of strict prayer. Since the rabbis looked upon the study of the Torah as an act of worship, the synagogue became under their influence a house of study as well. The reading and teaching of Scripture assumed a central and decisive role in Jewish public worship. Lectures and homilies given by recognized scholars became a regular instructional method which was built into the fabric of the service. But this was something more than a mere pedagogical device. Behind it lay the rabbinic conviction that worship must be linked to ethical service. Prayer that did not have a moral foundation would fall short of fulfilling the biblical injunctions. Learning to do God's will required constant study of the Torah, especially of the prophets, as well as of recent rabbinic interpretation.

The synagogue soon became a place of communal assembly. Courts of law met in its rooms, took testimony, administered oaths, and made judgments. Strangers to the community were welcomed into its hostel, the poor were given alms there, and community funds were administered by its councils. These broad communal and humanitarian functions were eventually so well integrated with the religious and educational programs that the synagogue became the supreme center of Jewish life.

The development of the Pharisees and the synagogal approach to Jewish religious life which we have just sketched is a far cry from the negative picture presented in the New Testament and traditional Christian catechesis. Through some knowledge of Jewish life in the intertestamental and post-biblical periods Christians can counter the distortions inherent in an apologetical approach. Knowledge of the spirit and attitudes of Pharisaic Judaism is important for Christians because all of the major branches within present-day Judaism in America owe their origin to Pharisaism, in spite of their particular differences. Pharisaism, with its stress on the people of Israel, also makes possible the modern phenomenon of the so-called secular Jew who does not belong to any of the established Jewish denominations but still considers himself very much a part of the community of Israel.

The New Testament describes several hostile encounters between Jesus and the Pharisees. They seem on several occasions to be bitter enemies of Jesus. Is this picture a pure fabrication of the Gospel writers? If not, what is the genesis of Jesus' disputes with the Pharisees?

Very likely some of the sharp denunciations of the Pharisees are the result of hostility between Church and the synagogue subsequent to the death of Jesus. Fr. Bruce Vawter, for example, insists that the polemic which the gospels wage against the Pharisees certainly cannot be separated from early Christian apologetics directed against the Jews.[7] Though, as we shall see below, the conflicts between Jesus and "the Pharisees" are rooted in actual disputes within first-century Palestinian Jewry about the meaning of the Law, they have been overstressed and simplified by the Gospel writers. As the early Christian community developed a growing awareness of its separation from Judaism, it lost interest in making distinctions among the various groups within Judaism and began to speak of Jews as such as its opponent. This process reaches its climax in the Gospel of John.

Another probable cause of the negative portrayal of the Pharisees in the New Testament is to be found in Pharisaism itself. Pharisaism was a movement more than a rigidly defined organization. It had room for diversity of thought within its general orientation. Inter-Pharisaic disputes apparently reached a high degree of tension in some cases. The Mishnah itself, which records the opinions of the Pharisaic rabbis, contains some passages which are as critical of Pharisees as anything found in the New Testament. Obviously these passages, coming from rabbis, are not meant as a blanket accusation against Pharisaism but against certain of its purported adherents.

The opposition and hostility within Pharisaism seems basically to have developed between two groups. This is the view at least of the noted Israeli scholar David Flusser.[8] He describes the emergence of a group among the Pharisees—the "Love" Pharisees, he calls them—who brought the charge against the "Veteran" Pharisees that they were serving God merely out of a dread of punishment and retribution rather than unconditional love. Jesus in his own teachings seems to have clearly sided with the new group of "Love" Pharisees. The point to be made, therefore, is that the New Testament's hostility to Pharisaism very likely is a hostility to a certain interpretation of Pharisaism which was being increasingly rejected and supplanted within the Jewish community at the time of Jesus rather than to Pharisaism as such. It should likewise be kept in mind that Jesus never encountered all of the Pharisees in his lifetime, but only a very small minority.

The internal divisions and consequent criticism that existed within Pharisaism at the time of Jesus should come as no great surprise to Christians. There are many works by Christian authors which bitterly castigate other Christians. And such criticism need not always be spoken in a vindictive spirit, but out of deep love for a movement which its in-group critics believe is not living up to its full potential. This was certainly the spirit in which the great prophets made their judgments and accusations against the people of Israel.

A cogent explanation of the New Testament disputes between Jesus and the Pharisees is offered by the historian-theologian, James Parkes. He contends that the real key to their relationship lies not in the wholesale condemnations of the Gospel of Matthew but in the simple narrative of Mark. Unlike the Sadducees and the Essenes, both Jesus and the Pharisees showed equal concern for the whole Jewish people. Jesus joined with the Pharisees in rejecting the drive of the Hellenistic Jews toward complete assimilation into the Hellenistic society. Jesus said he had come to fulfill the Torah, not destroy it through assimilation. It was precisely because their concerns were identical with those of Jesus that the Pharisees eventually developed a keen interest in Jesus. They were puzzled by what they saw and heard, but Mark's account reveals no great hostility. However, the Pharisees gradually began to look upon Jesus' independence of judgment as a danger in the confused socio-political situation of the time. The Pharisees were concerned with the absorption of Judaism by Hellenism and they insisted on a measure of separation by "building a fence around the Torah." They saw separation as the only guarantee of the survival of Israel's communal witness. Jesus, on the other hand, showed he was prepared to ignore the fence about the Sabbath (its basic observance was never at issue) and to justify his action with the generalization that the sabbath was made for man and not man for the sabbath. He did this to stress the need for personal submission to the Torah. The generalization itself is in line with Pharisaic principles.* But this type of independence was judged by them as too dangerous for the time. The popularity of Jesus increased the threat to national loyalty to Torah which the provisions for strict sabbath observance were intended to aid and insure. The Pharisees, says Parkes, had no choice but to oppose Jesus and to seek to undermine his influence. But they never sought to kill him and none of the Gospel accounts make any mention whatsoever of the Pharisees in their descriptions of the suffering and death of Jesus. It is essential to understand that the Pharisees could no more have simply accepted Jesus' teaching than he could have given in to them. His healing of a diseased hand on the sabbath was in itself not a crucial issue, but it was done deliberately by Jesus, according to Parkes, "as an assertion of the primacy of each man as person."[9]

Yet Parkes insists that Jesus never attempted, as far as we know, to bridge the gap between his own vision and the legitimate Pharisaic concern for the preservation of the community:

Within the divinely chosen community he proclaimed the divine concern with each man as person. It is for men to hold the two in a continuously destroyed and continuously re-created balance.

---

*"Scripture says, 'The sabbath is holy for *you*' (Ex. 31:14). This means it is given to *you* [man], not you to the sabbath" Talmud: Yoma 85b.

Jesus did not attempt to resolve the tension for us. He challenged only to recognize that it existed.[10]

After the encounter with the Pharisees over the observance of the sabbath laws, Mark continues to present Jesus teaching and healing with occasional arguments with the Pharisees and others. But from the beginning of his journey to the region of Caesarea Philippi, Parkes says the main thrust of Jesus' mission in Mark has changed. His own destiny and its continuing effect upon his followers moves into the center of the picture. And it is this "continuing effect" which became the *raison d'être* of the Christian Church. For, through his disciples, it was to be communicated to the entire world.[11]

According to Parkes, the tension between Jesus and the Pharisees was a creative one, reflecting the dual inheritance of humanity, the tension between person and community. There was no inherent need for a complete separation to occur. There was room within Pharisaic Judaism for varied opinion as the differing schools, such as those of Hillel and Shammai, clearly testify.* And for a time after the death of Jesus, the disciples still considered themselves a Jewish sect, for in the Book of Acts we find some of them continuing to go to synagogue. Yet Christianity's new teachings could be absorbed into the Jewish framework only with great difficulty. Unity was not totally impossible, but the separation is not surprising in retrospect. The tragedy of the split has been the reduction of creative tension into stark opposition, a situation from which neither community has benefited.

The complete separation of the two communities has also permitted Christians to frequently identify themselves solely with the "heroes" of the New Testament narrative and to see the Jews solely as the "villains." Carried over into a contemporary context this may too easily make an individual Christian feel that he is automatically superior to any Jew regardless of the depth of his

---

*"The words of both schools are the words of the living God, but the law follows the ruling of the school of Hillel because the Hillelites were gentle and modest, and studied both their own opinions and the opinions of the other school, and humbly mentioned the words of the other school before theirs" (Talmud: Erubin, 13b).

personal religious commitments. And even in those cases when Christian textbooks have stressed that all people are responsible through their sins for the death of Christ, as was the case in some of the passages cited in previous chapters, Christian identification with Jews is restricted solely to the negative role of "sinner" and not viewed in any positive context.

NEW ATTITUDES TOWARD THE CRUCIFIXION AND DEATH OF JESUS

The second major problem area in Christian-Jewish relations revealed in the textbook analyses was the blame frequently placed upon the Jewish people as a whole for the death of Jesus. Historians have found that the doctrine of deicide was never officially proclaimed by a Church council or by a papal decree. Yet it was widespread among the Christian masses since the time of the early Church and Church authorities rarely took any steps to curb its influence. This charge has led to a history of bitter persecution of Jews by Christians. Most of this terrible history does not appear in textbooks dealing with the history of the Church. Thus, most Catholics are simply uninformed about the long tradition of Christian anti-Semitism, while most Jews are well aware of it. While the accusation has on the whole disappeared from Catholic teaching, its past effects ought to be made known to students in the course of their history and religion studies in order to set Christian-Jewish relations in their proper perspective.[12]

Vatican Council II, in its *Declaration on the Relationship of the Church to Non-Christian Religions,* rejected the accusation of deicide against the Jews and the consequent charge of the punishment of perpetual wandering found in popular Christianity and still present in some of the materials examined in the St. Louis University studies:

True, the Jewish authorities and those who followed their lead pressed for the death of Christ; still, what happened in his passion cannot be charged against all the Jews, without distinction, then alive, nor against the Jews of today. Although the Church is the new people of God, the Jews should not be presented as rejected or accursed by God, as if this followed from the Holy Scriptures. All should see to it, then, that in catechetical work or in the preaching of the Word of God they do not teach anything that does not conform to the truth of the Gospel and the spirit of Christ. . . . Besides, as the Church has always held and holds now, Christ underwent his passion and death freely, because of the sins of men and out of infinite love, in order that all may reach salvation. It is, therefore, the burden of the Church's preaching to proclaim the cross of Christ as the sign of God's all-embracing love and as the fountain from which every grace flows.[13]

The conciliar statement on the Jews does not deal in detail with the events leading up to Jesus' death. Modern historians and Scripture scholars have concluded with considerable foundation that Jesus' death was the result of collaboration between the Roman governor and a handful of Jewish leaders who ruled occupied Palestine for the imperial government. These Jewish leaders are denounced with great vehemence in Jewish literature itself for the injustices they perpetrated against their own people for the sake of personal gain. The Pharisaic revolution was, in part, directed against these leaders. The conciliar statement also fails to come to grips with the impression left by many passages in the New Testament that the Jews are collectively responsible for the death of Jesus. This is especially true of the use of the term "Jews" in the Gospel of John. In working with Catholic teachers I have found a great deal of confusion on this point. They are aware of the conciliar statement, but are uncertain how this statement relates to the accounts of Jesus' death recorded in the Gospel narratives. It is imperative, therefore, that in presenting materials about the crucifixion and death of Jesus teachers make use of the Vatican statement plus recent scholarly findings that provide an appropriate setting for understanding the New Testament accounts.[14] Certain critical passages in particular require background explanations. Particularly in the Gospel of John:

John 18:14—It was Caiaphas who had suggested to the Jews, "It is better for one man to die for the people."

This passage no doubt expresses apprehension on the part of Caiaphas that the Romans might suspect Jesus was planning a revolt against Rome. The situation in Jerusalem was very tense at this time, especially with the added crowds who were present for the Passover celebration. Pilate's presence in Jerusalem was already a sign that the imperial authorities were somewhat displeased with the manner in which the high priests and their priestly associates were administering Jewish affairs. The Romans were very intent on preserving order at almost any cost in their colonies. They could tolerate ideological differences as long as these did not affect the social order. If the Romans thought that Jesus might incite a group of Jews to rebellion, they might retaliate by imposing even harsher conditions upon the Jewish community. In this process Annas and Caiaphas and the small ruling Jewish elite would undoubtedly be removed and very likely be punished. Thus they were quite willing to sacrifice Jesus to safeguard their own favored position.

John 18:31—Pilate said, "Take him yourselves, and try him by your own law." The Jews answered, "We are not allowed to put a man to death."

This passage is only one example of the attempt by the Jewish political leadership to make clear to the Romans that Jesus was guilty of political subversion. The charge they made against him was that he had proclaimed himself "king of the Jews," that he had challenged Rome's political authority in Palestine. With such a charge they were correct in insisting, in answer to Pilate, that they could not try Jesus. For under the colonial arrangement with Rome, the Jewish authorities could try and punish only religious violations, not political cases. It is quite possible that the high priests did not want to accept Pilate's subsequent offer to try Jesus for a religious offense because they feared Pilate was playing politics with them. If they accepted his offer, they might very well be accused of committing a man on a political charge, something they had no legal right to do. On the other hand, if they were to acquit Jesus, they might be accused of releasing a political offender against the Romans. In spite of the fact that Pilate comes out rather clean in the New Testament accounts, we know from ancient writers such as Josephus and Philo that he was a cruel tyrant easily capable of such a plot. Nowhere in the New Testament accounts do we have a clear-cut sentence handed down upon Jesus by the Jewish leaders. His official condemnation to death comes from Pilate.

John 18:40—At this they shouted: "Not this man," they said, "but Barabbas." Barabbas was a brigand.

The size of the "crowd" which chose the release of Barabbas rather than Jesus must not be exaggerated. There is no question here of any mass outpouring of the Jerusalem population. It may be, though this is far from certain, that the people who called for Barabbas' release were Zealots or members of the so-called Fourth Philosophy. These people advocated the violent overthrow of Roman rule. Some of them were perhaps disillusioned with Jesus, having believed at one time that he might develop into one of their leaders. We do know that at least one of the apostles, Simon, had Zealot connections. It is possible that Judas also may have had Zealot leanings. Barabbas was not a "robber" in the ordinary sense of the term. The word used to describe him in the Greek text referred to political prisoners from the group who advocated violent action against the Roman government. Thus the Zealots, disillusioned with Jesus, may simply have taken the opportunity to have one of their own released from prison.

John 19:7—"We have a law," the Jews replied, "and according to that law he ought to die, because he has claimed to be the Son of God."

The first impression one receives in reading this passage is that Jesus is being accused of theological heresy. What "law" this passage refers to, however, remains somewhat of a mystery. It very likely refers to Roman law, to which the Jewish leadership is trying to demonstrate its full allegiance, rather than to any Jewish religious law. Scholars have been unable to find any religious law, either in the Scriptures or in the Talmud, that prescribed capital punishment for a person who claimed to be the "Son of God." The term at that time simply did not carry the same type of theological meaning it came to have in later Christianity. "Son of God" was a common expression among Jews who followed a type of apocalyptic theology. In the book of Enoch the term is frequent. As used in this passage, the term "Son of God" must have appeared to constitute some form of challenge to Roman authority over the Jews rather than to imply theological heresy.

John 19:15—"Here is your king," Pilate said to the Jews. "Take him away, take him away!" they said. The chief priests answered, "We have no king except Caesar." So in the end Pilate handed him over to be crucified.

It is important to note in this passage how the kingship charge is crucial in the final decision by Pilate to crucify Jesus and how the chief priests wish to avoid any impression that they have accepted Jesus as their king. And the punishment that is ordered—crucifixion—indicates a political, not a religious, sentence inflicted by the state rather than by the Jewish leadership. The Jewish authorities could only put people to death on a religious charge. And in such cases the punishment was stoning, as we see in the case of Stephen in the Book of Acts. Crucifixion was a Roman, not a Jewish, form of punishment. The charge of kingship against Jesus is something found only in the passion narratives and is never brought up in any of his disputes with the Pharisees. All this goes to prove that, however some Jews may have disagreed with Jesus theologically, it was not because of his theological views as such that he was put to death. It was only insofar as his preaching on love and justice constituted a threat to the intolerant Jewish clique running Jerusalem for the Romans, and indirectly to the preservation of order in the city, that the authorities decided he must be put to death. It is the prerogative of later Christian theology to speculate on the meaning of Jesus' death for the salvation of men. But such reflections cannot be separated from everything Jesus taught and did during his lifetime, nor can it imply that the Jewish people as a whole put Jesus to death because they disagreed with him on religious grounds. His crucifixion and death as such was a political act on the part of Rome and the Jewish priestly elite. It was not only Jesus who suffered at the hands of this Roman-Jewish collaboration. The Jewish religio-political establishment was being challenged by both the Pharisees and the Zealots, each in their own way trying to bring it down because of the hardships it was imposing upon the Jewish people. A Jewish historian, Ellis Rivkin, describes the situation in the following way:

The question of "Who crucified Jesus?" should therefore be replaced by the question, "What crucified Jesus?" What crucified Jesus was the destruction of human rights, Roman imperialism, selfish collaboration. What crucified Jesus was a type of regime which, throughout history, is forever crucifying those who would bring human freedom, insight, or a new way of looking at man's relationship to man. Domination, tyranny, dictatorship, power and disregard for the life of others were what crucified Jesus. If there were among them Jews who abetted such a regime, then they too shared the responsibility. The mass of Jews, however, who were so bitterly suffering under Roman domination that they were to revolt in but a few years against its tyranny, can hardly be said to have crucified Jesus. In the crucifixion, their own plight of helplessness, humiliation and subjection was clearly written on the cross itself. By nailing to the cross one who claimed to be the Messiah to free human beings, Rome and its collaborators indicated their attitude toward human freedom."[15]

John 19:21-22—So the Jewish chief priests said to Pilate, "You should not write 'king of the Jews,' but 'This man said: I am king of the Jews.' " Pilate answered, "What I have written, I have written."

The final charge against Jesus is clear in the placard placed at the top of the cross. He was condemned for political sedition. The chief priests tried to get Pilate to change the phrasing for fear that Pilate might use it as a weapon to punish them and the Jewish populace on the charge of failing in their full loyalty to Caesar.

John 19:25—When the soldiers had finished crucifying Jesus they took his clothing and divided it into four shares, one for each soldier.

In this passage we have further confirmation of the view that
Jesus was put to death as a political offender. The property of
those executed on a religious charge was given by law to their
families. But anyone put to death for political reasons forfeited
his property to the state. Though not mentioned in John's Gospel,
the so-called "thieves" crucified with Jesus were in fact political
prisoners and not simply "robbers." Jesus was executed at a site
where political prisoners were being put to death by Rome with
regular frequency.

Finally, a word should be said about the blanket use of the
term "Jews" in the fourth Gospel. John wrote this Gospel for an
Hellenistic audience when the hostility between the Church and
the synagogue was already a major problem. This Gospel, as well
as the other Gospels, has a certain polemical quality. But added
to this is the fact that John's non-Jewish readers simply had no
idea of the various groups within Judaism at the time of Jesus. So
John simplifies matters and refers to the enemies of Jesus as "the
Jews." In so doing he left the tragic impression that it was the
Jews as such who opposed Jesus when, in fact, the masses of the
Jewish people shared a common enemy with Jesus, as the quotation from Dr. Rivkin cited above clearly illustrates. And as we
have seen in the examination of Catholic instructional materials,
John's blanket use of the term "Jews" was unfortunately repeated
by many of the textbook authors.

To conclude this section, modern biblical scholarship has
shown quite convincingly that the death of Jesus was not a plot
engineered by the general Jewish populace. As Fr. Bruce Vawter
has insisted, "there seems to be no doubt that Jewish responsibility has been heightened at the expense of the Roman. . . . In
particular, the governor Pontius Pilate as portrayed in the Gospels appears to be credited with a greater degree of disinterested
justice in his makeup than other historical sources concerning him
would cause us to suspect."[16] Paradoxically, the Gospel of John,
which has caused some of the greatest obstacles to Jewish-Christian understanding because of its blanket use of the term "the

Jews," most clearly places direct blame on Pilate and Rome for Jesus' death. John alone of the evangelists speaks of Roman intervention from the very beginning of the passion story with Jesus' arrest (cf. John 18:3). But Fr. Vawter also goes on to say that a factual history of the trial and death of Jesus has to be reconstructed rather than read from the Gospels. That is what we have tried to do in this chapter. A great deal of vital background material is missing from the Gospel narratives as they now stand. It must be supplied through auxiliary readings and commentaries. This situation also makes it almost impossible for even the very best of passion plays to entirely avoid a travesty of the Gospel story. We cannot obtain a fully accurate picture of the trial and death of Jesus from reading the Gospels alone. This is the clear conclusion of the vast majority of modern biblical scholars. It must also become a central guideline for the teacher in the presentation of the crucifixion story in the classroom.

NEW ATTITUDES TOWARD THE TWO COVENANTS

The relationship between the Old and New Testaments is the third of the major distortions of Judaism uncovered by the St. Louis studies. Further elaboration of the exact nature of this relationship still awaits the work of contemporary theologians, but enough study has been done on the subject to eliminate many of the stereotypes that have been commonplace in Catholic education.

The conciliar statement on the Jews from Vatican Council II, though not completely satisfactory in this regard, makes significant inroads against the stereotypes which have pictured post-biblical Judaism as a fossilized religion having no real meaning or value after the coming of Jesus, and which have often contrasted the Old Testament as a book of strict justice and legalism with the New Testament as a book marked by love and freedom:

The Church, therefore, cannot forget that she received the revelation of the Old Testament through the people with whom God in his inexpressible mercy concluded the ancient covenant. Nor can she forget that she draws sustenance from the root of that well-cultivated olive tree onto which have been grafted the wild shoots, the Gentiles, making both one in himself. The Church keeps ever in mind the words of the apostle about his kinsmen: "Theirs is the sonship and the glory and the covenants and the law and the worship and the promises; who have the fathers, and from whom is Christ according to the flesh" (Rom. 9:4-5). . . . God holds the Jews most dear for the sake of their fathers; he does not repent of the gifts he makes or of the calls he issues—such is the witness of the apostle. In company with the prophets and the same apostle, the Church awaits that day, known to God alone, on which all peoples will address the Lord in a single voice and "serve him shoulder to shoulder" (Soph. 3:9; cf. Is. 66:23; Ps. 65:4; Rom. 2:11-32).[17]

While this statement does not do full justice to the particular, continuing contribution of Judaism to mankind, it tempers in a significant way previous Catholic attitudes. We need to analyze more fully, however, the impression often left in Christian instruction that love is unique to the New Testament, and to offer some indication of how the relationship between Judaism and Christianity may be understood today.

The love-justice dichotomy which Christians have relied upon with great frequency to contrast their faith with Judaism has not wholly disappeared from the present scene. It can appear in very subtle ways. There is, for example, a song currently in wide use in folk Masses which speaks of Jesus having given us "a *new* command, that we should love our fellow man." The implication is that the primacy of love was first prescribed by Jesus rather than inherited from his Jewish background. His great commandment of love (Mt. 22:34-40) is taken right out of Yahweh's instruction to Moses in the Book of Leviticus (Chapter 19), and the same spirit is found in such books as Genesis, Exodus, Deuteronomy, the Psalms, and the Prophets. And the concrete expression of this love found in Jesus' deeds and preaching (especially in the beatitudes of the Sermon on the Mount) are an expression of the ethos that pervaded Pharisaic Judaism as it attempted to complete the Deuteronomic reform and incorporate the challenges of the Prophets into the structures of Jewish life. Rabbi Hillel's question

"If I am only for myself, what do I amount to?" is a spirit shared by both Jesus and Paul with rabbinic Judaism. Knowledge of the Old Testament (better called the Hebrew Bible) and of the intertestamental period is essential if the New Testament is to be understood in all its richness. Many of the attitudes and teachings of Jesus cannot be fully appreciated without a knowledge of the Jewish teachings upon which they rely. Judaism is the very foundation of the New Testament. But the full import of this foundation frequently will not come through if a person confines his study only to the New Testament. The New Testament has not simply absorbed all that was good and relevant in the Hebrew Bible. It presumed immersion in the Hebrew Bible and intertestamental Judaism on the part of the reader as the background for its message. The Hebrew Bible remains a living document for contemporary Christians, one that is vital for their own self-understanding. Nor must the impression be left that only biblical Judaism is of interest to Christians. Just as the fundamental Christian attitudes found in the New Testament have taken on varied forms and applications in the history of the Church, so too have Jewish traditions continued to grow and develop into our own time. It is important to know how contemporary Jews give expression to their traditions today, for Christians also share in those traditions.

An understanding of the two covenants of Sinai and Calvary may well be the crucial question in Jewish-Christian relations today. The outright distortions of Judaism in the past in Christian education can be corrected by a study of history. But what about the overriding impression in the *New* Testament that Christianity has totally superseded Judaism? It is the *New* Israel; it has a *New* Covenant and a *New* Moses. What then remains the role of Judaism in the *New* Age? Is it nothing more than an old wine sack? Has the Sinaitic covenant been replaced? Most Christian scholars have assumed so, but there are some who disagree. Among these is James Parkes, who argues that both covenants are necessary, because each speaks to man in a different aspect of his being: Calvary to man as individual, ignoring natural boundaries, Sinai to man as social being, existing in a natural community.

109

Parkes attempts to delineate the essentials of both covenants. The truths which make what he calls the Sinaitic revelation revolve around five crucial areas.[18] The first is the acceptance of a life which looks outward to the world because it looks inward to God. The declaration of the first commandment is the ultimate sanction on which are built the relations between men. But this life, and here lies the second point, is viewed as a unity. There is no division between the secular and the religious. Man, even as a sinner, still lives in the city of God, for there is no other place in which he could live. Third, human life means life in community. It is in community that men fulfill the will of God, not by the constant repetition of noble principles, but by the framing of just laws, honestly and courageously administered:

The revelation of Sinai was the perfect channel of the power which flows from the one God to men as members of the natural communities. Today we call them states, or local governments. Judaism is not a church; it is essentially a religion of a total natural community.[19]

The fourth emphasis in the Sinaitic revelation is the insistence that there is no viable law for man or society except the law of God. It is at this point, Parkes claims, that we see the fundamental need for the doctrine of growth and interpretation that later caused the schism between the Pharisees and the Sadducees. Finally, Sinai shows that there falls on each generation the responsibility for interpreting the will of God for its own time. No generation can simply rely on the interpretation of its predecessors, even on the written Torah, for God speaks directly to it against the background of its special needs and problems. Here lie the roots of the whole Talmudic system.

The revelation that was Calvary[20] adds a new dimension to Sinai. But this addition is complementary, not contradictory, to the first revelation. The teachings of Jesus could not have been given in any other environment than that of the Jewish community. Jewish society and its values are so completely presupposed in everything Jesus said and did that no direct references to them were required on his part. What he had to say about God and man would have been understood nowhere except in a Jewish context. Calvary concerns the sphere of the individual while Sinai centers around the community:

That highest purpose of God which Sinai reveals to men in community, Calvary reveals to man as an end in himself. The difference between the two events, both of which are incarnations of God, expressions of the infinite in the finite, of the eternal in the world of space and time, lies in the fact that the first could not reach fulfillment by only a brief demonstration of a divine community in action. The second, on the other hand, could not attain fulfillment except by a life lived under human conditions from birth to death.[21]

The revelation of Calvary did not replace Sinai, nor could Sinai simply absorb it and remain unchanged. In the life and teachings of Jesus the earlier revelation and the new revelation stand together in creative tension with one another. In the Christian concern with man as person, nothing is taken away from the power or meaning of the working out in history of the revelation of Sinai. Sinai did not mark the beginning of human concern with the moral problems of men in society. Behind Sinai were centuries of experience which were both human discoveries and divine revelations. What occurred at Sinai was the full development of a long and slow growth in man's understanding of community, even though it took centuries to realize the full extent of Sinai, and it remains difficult to define the complete meaning of that revelation today. In the same manner, the stress on the individual that had been growing in Judaism, since the exile, increased no doubt by Hellenistic contacts (especially at Alexandria), attained its full development with Calvary and has been subject to interpretation ever since:

The divine plan for human society is given its full meaning when the divine plan for man as person is revealed within it. In Jesus the ultimate unity is not destroyed; Paul still struggles to maintain it; but in the complex setting of first-century life the two halves broke apart, and the beginning of the second century witnessed two religions confronting each other—Judaism and Chris-

111

tianity.[22]

Judaism and Christianity are inextricably linked together as equals, for the tension that exists between them is rooted in the perennial and inevitable experience of tension in ordinary human life between man as social being and man as person, as an ultimate value in himself, as one formed in the likeness of God:

Man as citizen must be concerned with the attainable; as person he is concerned with the unattainable; as citizen he must perpetually seek a compromise, for he is dependent on his neighbor's acceptance; as person he must often refuse compromise; as citizen he is concerned with the impersonal, and must not let personal considerations warp his judgment; as person he approaches every other person as one "for whom Christ died" who must be made to observe no other ends. The tension extends through the whole of life and to matters of everyday concern, and it will endure so long as the world endures.[23]

Parkes is against the use of the term "salvation history" as a description of Jewish history, a term popular in recent Christian catechesis. It implies, he believes, something set apart from the regular processes of human life and reasoning. The Sinaitic revelation is embedded in ordinary, everyday history. For this reason the Jews today remain incapable of being fitted into the modern demand for a strict separation between a religion and a people.

Parkes' affirmation of the continuing validity and special mission of Judaism is shared by several other Christian scholars. Fr. Gregory Baum, for example, has insisted that even on the basis of the New Testament, the believing Christian must affirm that the Jewish religion has a positive place in God's plan for universal salvation.[24] Likewise it is wrong, in his view, to look upon Judaism simply as a precursor of Christianity.[25] Rather it must be recognized that while present-day Judaism is founded upon scriptural revelation and nourished by it, it has become, through an intricate history and a great variety of factors, a religion in its own right. While closely related to Christianity and enjoying a common patrimony with Christianity, Judaism is a religion possessing its own role and mission. The destiny of Judaism is not simply to disappear and give way to Christianity; Judaism continues to exercise a positive role in God's plan of salvation.

The Catholic theologian Dr. Monika Hellwig takes much the same approach as Fr. Baum to the question of the two covenants. She begins her approach to the relationship between Judaism and Christianity with the biblical view, expressed in the covenants of Adam and Noah, that all men are part of the universal covenant God has made with mankind and which is identified with the order of creation.[26] The Sinai and Calvary covenants are specifications of this one basic covenant. From this point of view Christians are seen to enjoy participation with Jews (and, though in radically different senses, with Islam and other faith communities) in a covenant made by God with all men and fully to be completed in the kingdom of promise which all the communities strive after and hope for but glimpse only darkly in symbols. That is a fact of history which cannot be erased even if all the Jews in the world were to be eradicated. How Christians and Jews are to find and explain their own complementarity within this covenant is a matter of interpretation with which Christian theologians still must grapple. But Christians have to assert quite clearly that both they *and* the Jewish people continue to witness and develop important aspects of the one basic covenant God has made with mankind. Thus it is inaccurate for the Christian educator to present the New Testament as totally supplanting the so-called "Old" Testament in the manner we have discovered in the textbooks examined by the St. Louis research team.

We must look at both Christianity and Judaism as essential for the ultimate fulfillment of mankind. Until there appears the way by which both can fulfill their respective roles together without losing their own essential nature, each must fulfill its own part alone and bring the insights of its own tradition to bear on the problems of the modern world. A Jewish scholar, Dr. Irving Greenberg, expresses well this spirit of the sharing of roles by Christianity and Judaism:

There are indeed men who are willing to live side by side until the end of days who do so because they are fully confident that the Messiah, when he comes, will confirm their rightness all along.

113

Of course, it is a step forward to live together until that time. But even here, we may underrate the love and wonder of the Lord. I have often thought of this as a kind of nice truism. Let us wait until the Messiah comes. Then we can ask him if this is his first coming or his second. Each of us could look forward to a final confirmation. A friend, Zalman Schachter, taught me that perhaps I was a bit too narrow in my trust in God with this conception. He wrote a short story in which the Messiah comes at the end of days. Jews and Christians march out to greet him and establish his reign. Finally they ask if this is his first or second coming. To which the Messiah smiles and replies, "No comment". . . . Perhaps we will then truly realize that it was worth it all along for the kind of life we lived along the way.[27]

The obligation of the Christian teacher is to make clear to the student the continuing validity of Judaism as a religion and its important contributions to mankind, to show him that the old stereotypes about the total absorption of Judaism by Christianity are wholly unwarranted. At the same time the teacher must frankly admit to the student that it may take Christian theologians quite some time to work out a new positive statement on the interrelationship of the two faith-communities, since Christianity has for so long a time defined itself in terms of the culmination of Judaism.

FOOTNOTES

1. "Christian Education and the Image of the Pharisees," reprinted from *Religious Education,* November-December, 1960, by the American Jewish Committee.
2. Cf. David Flusser, "A New Sensitivity in Judaism and the Christian Message," in *Encounter Today,* Autumn 1969, pp. 123-133 and Ellis Rivkin, "The Internal City," *Journal for the Scientific Study of Religion,* Spring 1966, pp. 225-240.
3. Cf. Ellis Rivkin, "The Parting of the Ways," in Lily Edelmann (ed.), *Face to Face: A Primer in Dialogue,* Washington: B'nai B'rith Adult Jewish Education, pp. 33-41; Asher Finkel, *The Pharisees and the Teacher of Nazareth. A Study of Their Background, Their Halachic and Midrashic Teachings, The Similarities and Differences,* Leiden: Brill, 1964; Frederick Grant, "Paul the Pharisee," in *Roman Hellenism and the New Testament,* New York: Charles Scribner's Sons, pp. 132-147.

4. *Sanhedrin,* IV: 5, as quoted in Ellis Rivkin, *op. cit.,* p. 233.
5. *Ibid.,* p. 234.
6. Stuart Rosenberg, "Contemporary Renewal and the Jewish Experience," paper delivered to the 1968 International Conference of Christians and Jews, York University, Toronto, Canada, p. 3.
7. Bruce Vawter, "Are the Gospels Anti-Semitic?" in *Journal of Ecumenical Studies,* Summer 1968, p. 485.
8. David Flusser, *op. cit.,* p. 127.
9. James Parkes, *The Foundations of Judaism and Christianity,* London: Vallentine-Mitchell, p. 177.
10. *Ibid.*
11. *Ibid.,* p. 179.
12. For a brief history of anti-Semitism, teachers may consult Edward Flannery, *The Anguish of the Jews,* New York: Macmillan, 1965.
13. *Declaration on the Relationship of the Church to Non-Christian Religions,* Huntington, Indiana: Our Sunday Visitor Press, p. 6. For an analysis of the development of the conciliar statement on the Jews, the various modifications and a Jewish critique, cf. Arthur Gilbert, *The Vatican Council and the Jews,* Cleveland: World Publishing Co., 1968.
14. Cf. Bruce Vawter, *op. cit.;* Dominic Crossan, "Anti-Semitism and the Gospel," in *Theological Studies,* 1965, pp. 189-214; Joseph A. Fitzmeyer, S.J., "Anti-Semitism and the Cry of 'All the People,' " in *Theological Studies,* 1965, pp. 667-671; Bernhard E. Olson, "The Crucifixion: The Jew and the Christian," reprinted from *Religious Education,* July-August, 1963, by The American Jewish Committee; Solomon Zeitlin, *Who Crucified Jesus?* New York: Bloch Publishing Co., 1964.
15. Ellis Rivkin, "The Parting of the Ways," *op. cit.,* p. 37.
16. Bruce Vawter, *op. cit.,* p. 486.
17. *Declaration on the Relationship of the Church to Non-Christian Religions, op. cit.,* pp. 5-6.
18. James Parkes, *Judaism and Christianity,* Chicago: University of Chicago Press, pp. 26-27.
19. "The End of the Way," 1966 International Conference of Christians and Jews, Newnham College, Cambridge, Cf. *Encounter Today,* Summer, 1967, pp. 90-93.
20. Parkes uses the term "Calvary" as a symbol of the life and death of Jesus.
21. *Judaism and Christianity,* p. 30.
22. *The Foundations of Judaism and Christianity,* p. 131.
23. *Ibid.*
24. Gregory Baum, O.S.A., "Jewish-Christian Dialogue," in *The Month,* November 1967, p. 242.
25. *Ibid.,* p. 244.
26. Monika Hellwig, "Christian Theology and the Covenant of Israel," in *Journal of Ecumenical Studies,* Winter 1970, p. 44.
27. Irving Greenberg, "The New Encounter of Judaism and Christianity," in *Barat Review,* June 1968, pp.124-125.

CHAPTER 7

CONCLUSIONS

In previous chapters we have discussed a number of themes which frequently occasion negative or distorted treatment of Jews and Judaism in Catholic textbooks. In this concluding chapter we will explore some questions which are seldom touched upon in elementary or high school textbooks but which nevertheless have affected the historical relationship between the two faiths and still influence Catholic attitudes toward Jews and Judaism. We shall indicate some of the directions in which recent Catholic scholarship has been moving in order to come to grips with these questions.

PAUL AND JUDAISM

A particularly troublesome point in Christian-Jewish relations has been Paul's apparently passionate hostility to the Torah after his conversion. Since observance of the Torah was central to Jewish faith, the often vehement denunciations in the Pauline epistles, especially Galatians, of those Christian converts who maintained strict observance of the Torah has been viewed as a major cause

117

of severing of the early Church from its Jewish setting. Moreover, the incorporation of Paul's attacks on the law into the Sacred Scripture of Christianity undoubtedly maintained the tension between the two communities across the centuries.

Some of this apparent hostility on the part of Paul toward the Torah can be cushioned by a proper understanding of the background of these epistles. Most of Paul's condemnations of insistence on strict Torah observance occur in letters written to Gentile rather than Jewish converts. In not insisting on observance of the Torah Paul was simply following good rabbinic practice of the time which said that adherence to the Law was not to be imposed on Gentiles as a requisite for salvation. And if Paul believed that the messianic age (in the sense of the end of history) had really taken place, then he was simply following the rabbinic opinion that the Torah was meant to be observed while history continued, ceasing to have force in messianic times.

But placing Paul's comments in their Jewish setting still does not adequately account for the antagonism toward the Law in some Pauline passages. Some scholars have explained it on the grounds of Paul's own personal conversion, which gave him a sense of release from the Law, a sense of personal freedom which he wanted everyone else to share with him.[1] Recent biblical scholarship has indicated another possibility which provides a more positive context. The so-called "Judaizers" who are the principal targets of Paul's hostility were, according to some recent Pauline commentators, not converts from Judaism trying to retain their former practices and impose them on others as Christian obligations, but former Gentiles who for one reason or another had become deeply attached to the prescriptions of the Torah before or after their conversion.[2] Their approach to the Torah, however, was far more legalistic than the progressive forces in Judaism, especially the Pharisees, would have accepted. These new converts were, perhaps unwittingly, taking an approach to the Law which paralleled that of the Sadducees against whom the Pharisees, Paul included, had fought with great vigor. Thus, according to this interpretation, Paul's opposition to the "Judaizers" stems more from his Pharisaic Jewish background than from anything specifically Christian in his theology.

THE PROBLEM OF BIBLICAL TEXTS

Recent biblical and extra-biblical scholarship has done much to explain the antagonism which emerges from a simplistic reading of the New Testament by providing a contextual framework for understanding, say, Paul's attacks on the Law, or the struggle between Jesus and the Pharisees. Yet these explanations, essential as they are, and helpful as they have been in improving textbook presentations of critical events in the encounter between Judaism and Christianity, nevertheless point back to a major problem which remains a sore point between many sensitive Christians and Jews: the apparent anti-Semitism of the New Testament.

This is not to imply that the New Testament texts are anti-Semitic in an intentional sense, or that they condemn outright the Jewish people as a whole. Outstanding Scripture scholars such as Bruce Vawter have concluded that no general accusation of anti-Semitism can be leveled at the Gospels.[3] The Gospel narratives reflect true disputes over the meaning of the Law which were part and parcel of first-century Palestinian Judaism. Nonetheless, Fr. Vawter asserts that, read uncritically, this inter-Jewish hostility has provided an opening for a kind of anti-Semitism that the Gospels never intended.

While the possible negative impact of the controversial passages can be offset by appropriate background explanation in the classroom setting—hopefully by trained teachers and with the assistance of teachers' manuals prepared for this purpose—a major problem remains when these texts are read in the sacred setting of the official worship of the Church, where no background is generally given. Anyone who would deny this only has to go through the experience, as I have, of reading such texts during a liturgy at which Jews were present as guests. Some Catholic scholars have called for a retranslation of these texts which would eliminate the general use of the term "the Jews," for example, where the reference seems to be only to a particular Jewish group of the time.

Dr. Michael D. Zeik made this suggestion several years ago:

Historians are aware today that six of the eight million Jews then living, or fully three-fourths of them, lived outside of Palestine in Diaspora, and never so much as heard of Christ until some time after his death. It is evident, then, that the term "Jews" is used here as an "editorial-collective" noun. In much the same way, we say "the Russians did this," and "the Chinese did that," when we really mean that Brezhnev and Mao-Tse-tung, together with the ruling party members, did this or that.

Now the "editorial-collective" is commonly accepted today in modern journalism. Under ordinary circumstances it can probably be used without fear of deception or injustice. Unfortunately, the treatment of Jews by Christendom in past centuries, or by racists in this century, does not argue the presence of "ordinary circumstances." Extraordinary measures, it seems to me, are called for, if we are ever to wipe out this virus of hatred and blood-lust.[4]

A Protestant educator, Dr. Lee Belford, has made a similar suggestion:

What is the impact when Christians continue to hear Jews denounced as culprits in their holy Scriptures? Repetition of certain words upon our thinking is the key to effective propaganda. It does little good to try to explain the background; the impact of the oft-repeated phrase is too overwhelming. We affirm that all men are involved in guilt for the death of Christ and in the spirit of his love for all mankind. Yet we repeat phrases that have created a spirit of antipathy toward our brothers—those who have a special place in the economy of God. We are legalists and enemies of the Spirit. For some of us it is offensive to read the anti-Jewish statements that abound in the otherwise glorious Gospel of John and in the earliest history of the Church, the Acts of the Apostles. (For the statistician, there are 37 anti-Jewish statements in John; 38 in Acts.) What can be done about the matter? . . . .

If we admit that there are anti-Jewish statements in the Bible and that we are stuck with a text, would it not be preferable to use the word Judean for Jew where it appears in the New Testament? The word for Jews in Greek is *Ioudaioi*. A logical transliteration would be Judeans. Nelson's Bible Commentary of 1962 speaks of the possibility of substituting Judean for Jew and the suggestion has been reiterated in other sources as well, but the translators have done nothing about it. Jew is derived from the French "juif" which comes from the Old French "gui" which is derived from the Latin "judaeus." Our transliteration would be more accurate if we got a little closer to the Greek and Latin forms.[5]

On initial consideration this approach sounds attractive as a means of removing a major roadblock to better Christian-Jewish understanding. But Scripture scholars, who ultimately would be entrusted with the task of retranslation, do not appear to be optimistic about the prospects. Dr. Krister Stendahl of Harvard is of such a view.[6] He feels that the tension between the Church and the synagogue in the first century is of little surprise. The early Christian Church was a distinct and vigorous movement within Judaism, fierce in its criticism of other segments of Judaism. We have a parallel to this in the Dead Sea Scrolls, discovered several years ago. Here we find scathing and even hateful comments about the Jewish establishment in Jerusalem. The Jewish prophetic tradition contains similarly fierce expressions against "Judaism." The real problem, according to Dr. Stendahl, stems from the fact that the prophetic language fell into the hands of the Gentiles. Some of these Gentiles, especially those of Roman origin, had a history of anti-Semitism in their pre-Christian backgrounds. They were the people who generally put the finishing touches on the form of the New Testament documents. In their own search for identity they found meaning partly in the "no of the Jews" to Jesus Christ. Once the Jewish context and identification of the early Church disappeared, the inter-Jewish conflict statements were hardened into accusations against "the Jews," against the synagogue across the street, and against the people who claimed the same Scriptures but denied their completion in Jesus. Dr. Stendahl says that the consequence of this development is that the Christian Church had no "right" to the use of these prophetic Jewish statements once she had severed all her connections with Judaism. For in the new situation, without instead of within the Jewish community, these same words, even when repeated verbatim, take on an entirely new meaning.[7]

Carried into the concrete situation of today, Stendahl's suggestion would seem to dictate some attempt to remove certain texts from use at the eucharistic liturgy where they seem to continually receive at least tacit approbation from the Church. While the official texts would remain as they are, unless sound scholarship would seem to warrant a change (something most biblical scholars consider highly unlikely), there could simply be the deletion of certain particularly troublesome passages in the texts used for readings. Such "license" is an accepted part of the oral presentation of literature, and there seems little reason why it could not be applied in this situation. An official "reading" text might be drawn up by a committee of experts sensitive to Jewish-Christian problems to facilitate this modification in the text. The regular text could continue in use in writing and in the classroom where there is less of a sacred approbation given the material and where background explanations are possible.

Until such a "reading" text is produced, however, teachers can play an important role during the school year in keeping alert for particularly troublesome passages that might appear in the Sunday liturgy. Some brief explanation of these passages could be given by the teacher in the class nearest the Sunday on which the texts will be read. This is by no means the perfect solution. But it would be one way of providing the background to these passages which frequently cannot be given in the course of the liturgy itself.

Another way to combat the effect of these texts is the development of a positive appreciation of Judaism among Christian students. This would include the realization that Judaism did not cease to be creative and living after the rise of Christianity, but continued to develop many of the traditions of its biblical heritage in the light of new cultural situations. If it becomes apparent to Christian students that the Church has a great deal to learn spiritually and intellectually from the Jewish religious tradition, both in its biblical and its contemporary expression, the negative force of the New Testament texts in question will be greatly diminished and more likely understood in their proper historical context. A first important step in this process is the recent inclusion of readings from the Hebrew Bible in the regular Sunday liturgy of the

Church. Too often Christians have looked upon the Hebrew Bible as a mere prelude to the New Testament. Its morality and religious insights were considered inferior to those of the New Testament, and it was frequently assumed that whatever still retained value in the Hebrew Bible had been incorporated into the New Testament. Hearing the Hebrew Bible weekly at the liturgy may help Christians see for the first time the depth of religious expression found in the Hebrew Bible.

In our time, the Church is beginning to recover some of the heritage of Judaism which she has neglected since the war with Rome in 67-70 A.D. virtually destroyed the Jewish-Christian community in Palestine. Among recent Christian writers, there is a new interest in certain themes and religious values which have always been central to Judaism. Among these are:

1. *The Importance of History.* A major theme in Christian catechetical materials since Vatican Council II has been the notion of salvation history. While emphasis on this theme has sometimes left the erroneous impression that "salvation history" is somehow separate from ordinary "human" history, it has brought back into Christianity a distinctly Jewish theme. The early Church, deeply imbued with a Jewish sense of history, understood the coming of Jesus as the completion of history. Because the Messiah had come, Christians could enter the post-historical age. Paul, who expressed this view in his early epistles, began to modify it as the world around him continued to bear the marks of unredemption, but the change in his viewpoint was not fully developed by later theologians, and this lack had serious consequences for later Christian theology. The vital links between the earthly and divine realms, the sense of man's responsibility for the world, which were central to the Jewish spirit, were lost on the premise that history had already been completed in Jesus.

Today, Christians are aware that the messianic age of peace and justice described by Second Isaiah has still not arrived. Human history continues, and man still has much to learn and a great deal to accomplish. Rabbi Arthur Hertzberg, an outstanding contemporary Jewish scholar and a man deeply involved in

Christian-Jewish dialogue, poses the problem in this way:

Advanced Christians are confronting the unredeemed world. As they sit amidst the rubble of all the shattered hopes, including their own theological ones, advanced Christians are hoping to redeem the world by a new devotion to Jesus. This is a very "Jewish" stance, for we Jews have been in the business of living through and beyond tangible and intangible exiles and disasters from the very beginning of our experience. We know that all is never lost—but, for that matter, that all is never won, either. In the age of the concentration camps and the re-creation of a Jewish commonwealth in Israel we have known both the greatest despair and historic comfort. To be a Jew means to believe, and to wait.[8]

2. *Man's Responsibility for Creation.* Related to the importance of history is this theme, in which Yahweh charges man with the care of the world he has created. This theme has always been paramount in the teaching of Judaism. Man is in a genuine sense a partner, as well as a servant, of God. On this affirmation Judaism has never yielded. While Christianity has never denied this responsibility, its notion that history was completed and creation brought to perfection in Christ greatly diminished the seriousness of this sense of partnership as a basic human task. Jews have seen that man achieves his redemption through his care of God's creation. Frequently in the Christian understanding of how man attains salvation the impression has been given that creation could be bypassed. Because of Christ there now was a direct route to salvation. Salvation became a matter between the individual person and God. But a major theme in recent Christian theology has been the focus on the "secular city" and on evolution. In this perspective man has the responsibility of struggling to overcome the problems of the world and developing the consciousness of man. In so doing he is exercising his partnership with God and achieving his own salvation. Such an approach is very much in line with traditional Jewish thinking.

3. *Salvation in Community.* This aspect of Jewish existence is succinctly summarized by Rabbi Jacob J. Weinstein, who writes

that "the exaltation of the community in the sacred fellowship of man" forms one of the major features of the Jewish tradition:

Social responsibility is as high a value in the Jewish ethic as personal fulfillment. The two are in fact intertwined and utterly dependent one on the other. Consider the admonition from Pirké Avot: "Do not separate thyself from the community." Salvation is impossible outside of community. *If I am only for myself, what do I amount to?* Hillel's question has come down to the Jews of our day. The magnificent social welfare institutions of the Jewish community attest to this.[9]

The Hebrew Bible emphasizes this aspect of community with unmistakable clarity on numerous occasions. It is the community that will eventually be saved when the messianic age arrives. The individual will be saved only as part of the community. Though the Pharisees eventually come to insist strongly on the resurrection of each individual, this personal resurrection still had to await the salvation of the full community with the coming of the messianic age. Since the time of Vatican Council II the Church has begun to look at the notion of salvation much more from the Jewish perspective of community. The reintroduction by the Council of the term "people of God" as a description of the Church is one indication. The Church today is saying that we are our brother's keeper because our own salvation cannot be divorced from the destiny of our brother. This has been a consistent Jewish belief even if in the modern world it has been often expressed by Jews in secular forms. The kibbutz system in modern Israel is one expression of the Jewish sense of community.

4. *Man Is Not Basically Evil.* Since the time of St. Paul and the early Church Fathers, Christianity has looked upon man as a fallen creature. In part this was the result of the theological connection which developed between original sin and the Church's understanding of Jesus as the Savior. St. Augustine, in particular, was concerned with the sinful nature of man. Other Christian writers did attempt to modify Augustine's view, but his outlook generally prevailed in the Church. This image of man as inherent-

ly sinful never secured a firm foothold in normative Judaism. Judaism had another vision of human nature which revolved about the idea of two "yetzerim" (impulses) in man. the good impulse and the evil impulse. Both of these are under the dominion of man's human power. What is even more important, traditional Judaism recognized explicitly that the so-called evil impulse may be transposed into a higher key in order to honor God and serve the needs of men. Though admitting the risk of oversimplification, Rabbi Robert Gordis has described the difference between the traditional Christian and Jewish attitudes toward the nature of man in the following terms:

For traditional Christianity, man sins because he is a sinner; for traditional Judaism, man is a sinner because he sins.[10]

Christians are beginning to gravitate more and more in our day toward Judaism's more positive evaluation of man, especially in the area of sexual morality. Sex has always been looked upon as a higher value in Jewish religious tradition. This also holds true with respect to the place of family life.

The increased emphasis in recent Christian thought on these "Jewish" values and themes can help Christian students to better understand the roots and heritage of their faith. Whether or not it will help them to acquire an appreciation of the beauty and depth of Judaism will largely depend on how the material is presented. If, as has happened many times in the past, Christianity appropriates aspects of Jewish tradition and presents them as its own, it is questionable whether a more sympathetic understanding of Judaism will ensue.

Jewish religious traditions and celebrations are increasingly venerated in Catholic teaching today, but largely in terms of their value for enriching the Church's heritage and self-understanding, not their religious validity for Jews. The use of the term "the people of God" to describe the Church is a case in point; it represents a return to Jewish categories of thought and reveals the influence of the Hebrew Scriptures in the understanding of a covenanted people, but it also seems to deny—or at best ignore—God's enduring covenant with the Jewish people.

126

JUDAISM AND ISRAEL

In a report presented to the National Conference of Catholic Bishops in 1970, Father Edward H. Flannery, Executive Secretary of the Secretariat for Catholic-Jewish relations, noted the extent to which the state of Israel has become a major issue for Jewish-Christian relations:

Jews have in the vast majority identified with that state whether as a refuge from anti-Semitism, a new source of Jewish identity and survival, or as a Messianic fulfillment. They see Zionism as central to Judaism itself and essential not only to Israeli but also Jewish survival, and therefore as an ecumenical and a religious consideration which should be included in the dialogue. They have judged Christian coolness or silence with respect to Israel's peril, especially during the Six Day War, as indifference toward what they considered the possibility of another genocide, and have expressed their disappointment. The charge of silence has been taken into the dialogue with good results. Among other things, Christian dialogists have learned more of the intense bond uniting Jews to Israel, and Jews have learned some of the questions Christians have had on this subject.[11]

As previously noted, our preoccupation with American and Western European history has frequently led to neglect of other areas in both textbooks and teacher education. This has meant that we are relatively unprepared to deal with two different, but related, issues: the Middle East as an area of contemporary concern, and the relationship between Judaism and Israel. These subjects are complex; obviously they cannot be fully treated in this volume. However, no discussion of Christian-Jewish relations is complete without them. Some factual information may help provide a framework for teachers.

Two overwhelming events have shaped the consciousness of Jews in this century: the systematic slaughter of six million Jews, one and a half million of them children, during the Nazi period, and the creation of the state of Israel. While the two events may not be connected by historical necessity, they are deeply connected in the minds and hearts of most Jews. As a prominent Jewish scholar, Rabbi Leon Jick, puts it:

127

With the establishment of the state of Israel, Jewish history was once again transformed. The redemptive promise of the prophets, the resurrective experiences of ancient Israel was literally relived in our times: the dry bones rose and were restored to life. With this restoration, Jewish history was transformed from a chronicle of calamities to an epic of triumph over adversity. The horror of the holocaust could not be undone. But this horror was no longer that last word—not even the climax. . . .

The establishment of Israel, therefore, changed history for us. It restored to us not only a measure of confidence in the future of our own people, it resurrected our hope for mankind. It rekindled our anticipation that perhaps man can overcome evils and prevail over the demonic powers loose in the world. With the birth of Israel was reborn the prospect of Jewish history as a paradigm and the Jewish people as a model. . . . As in Israel's antiquity, the establishment of the particularist nation-state was the instrument through which the universalist mission was resuscitated.[12]

The modern political movement for the establishment of a Jewish national homeland had its beginnings during the famous Dreyfus affair in France at the end of the nineteenth century. Present at the trial of Dreyfus was an assimilated Jewish journalist named Theodore Herzl. Dreyfus' ordeal, and the waves of political anti-Semitism set off by the trial, convinced Herzl that emancipation had not succeeded in overcoming anti-Semitism. The ultimate solution he saw as political and national. The Jew must have a state of his own. Herzl clearly foresaw the possibility of a Nazi-type slaughter of the Jews taking place in Europe. Herzl interested other Jews in a plan for the creation of a Jewish national homeland, and a world Zionist organization was born in 1897. While other locations were initially considered, it soon became apparent that only Palestine, the ancient homeland of the Jews, could evoke the determination and self-sacrifice necessary to create a new homeland. A Jewish settlement was already in the Holy Land, one that had been there continuously from biblical times, but the land had been neglected for centuries under Turkish rule.

The Zionist movement pursued two courses: one, to purchase,

settle and develop the land through the labor of Jewish pioneers; second, to seek an internationally approved charter to set up a Jewish state. In a background paper, "The Foundations of the State of Israel,"[13] Father Flannery traces the juridical foundation of the state of Israel back to the Balfour Declaration, as expressed in an official letter from British Foreign Secretary Arthur Balfour to Lord Rothschild of England in 1917:

His Majesty's Government view with favor the establishment in Palestine of a national home for the Jewish people, and will use their best endeavors to facilitate the achievement of this object, it being clearly understood that nothing shall be done which may prejudice the civil and religious rights of existing non-Jewish communities in Palestine, or the rights and political status enjoyed by Jews in any other country.

The Balfour principle was ratified by other governments, including the United States, restated in several treaties and acquired effective international legal status when it was incorporated into the special mandate for Palestine awarded by the League of Nations to Great Britain.

The League of Nations also established the provisions under which more than a million square miles of territory were allocated to the Arab peoples for early independence. By 1947 this independence had been achieved by seven Arab states. (Currently, the Arab world includes eighteen independent states extending over 4,600,000 square miles with a population of some 113 million.)

As for Palestine itself, relying on the Balfour Declaration, Jews hoped for the whole of it, including some 45,000 square miles. But in actuality, the British took four-fifths of the land to create the Arab state of Transjordan in 1922.

In 1947, in the face of mounting Arab-Jewish conflict, Great Britain turned the question of Palestine over to the United Nations whose General Assembly voted to create a Jewish and an Arab state by partitioning the country. The partition plan, which recognized the national claims of both Jews and Palestinian Arabs, was the result of a study conducted by a United Nations

Special Committee on Palestine (UNSCOP). The plan was accepted by a vote of 33 to 13 with 10 abstentions. It was one of the few issues on which the United States and Soviet Russia have voted together.

On May 14, 1948, as the British withdrew, the new state of Israel issued its Declaration of Independence. But the Arab states defied the UN partition plan, and the armies of Egypt, Transjordan, Syria, Lebanon and Iraq marched against Israel. The territory that was to have been the Palestinian Arab state disappeared, most of it annexed by Transjordan (now Jordan), some of it taken over and administered militarily by Egypt, and some of it taken by Israel. The refugee problem was born.

Father Flannery concludes by acknowledging that the Arab-Israeli conflict is a "complex and tragic affair. There have been wrongs on both sides and on the side of the Great Powers, but Israel's juridical foundations, her right to exist and develop in peace cannot be questioned."[14]

Zionism has frequently been characterized as secular and socialistic. There is only a partial truth in this depiction. Many of the early Zionist leaders abandoned some of the practices and beliefs of traditional Judaism, among them the expectation of a personal Messiah who would restore a Jewish state in Palestine. The homeland, they said, must be created by the dedication and labor of Jews themselves. Undoubtedly, the Zionist movement gained some impetus from the growth of nationalist feelings throughout Europe at the time, when many groups were demanding the right of national self-determination. Most of the Zionist leaders believed in some form of democratic socialism, which was translated into the concrete through the establishment of *kibbutzim,* the communal settlements which formed the backbone of Jewish settlement in Palestine. In the *kibbutzim,* the land, equipment and produce were—and still are—owned in common by all members, and the community is governed by democratic rule.

Many Zionists were devoted to the idea of labor—particularly agricultural labor—as having a saving effect on the human spirit. Jews had been prohibited from owning land in many parts of Europe; they had lost the sense of relatedness to the land which was part of their biblical heritage. By reclaiming the land through their own labor, they would also be reclaiming their own dignity. These people, known as Labor Zionists, were the counterparts of the East European Jews in America who played such an important role in the American labor union movement. There were also Zionists who had a specifically religious orientation. Outstanding among them were Achad-ha-Am and Martin Buber.

To explain the Zionist movement, even in its secular manifestations, as simply another form of modern political nationalism does serious injustice both to the diversity of motivation within the Zionist movement and to the depth of the longing for a return to Zion in the Jewish religious tradition.

For the land of Israel—Zion—has been a continuing source of spiritual longing and anticipation, as both symbol and reality, for the Jewish people and for their capacity for regeneration. In the Psalms God is called the king of Zion and Zion is proclaimed as the "city of the great king" (Ps. 48:3). Zion has continued to retain this sacred significance for Jews. The land of Israel is looked upon not merely as a holy land, but as *the* holy land. Unlike Christians, Jews have been less attached to religious shrines in the Holy Land than to the land itself. In all their prayers and religious devotions the aspirations and the hope of the Jewish people in exile remained intimately bound up with it. All of these associations with the land continue to remain strong in the people of Israel. This not only makes their relationship to Israel unique, but also explains why the idea of Zionism has remained a remarkable force for Jewish renewal. Martin Buber has summarized this Jewish feeling in the following way:

This land was at no time in the history of Israel simply the property of the people; it was always at the same time a challenge to make of it what God intended to have made of it. . . . It was a consummation that could not be achieved by the people of the land on its own but only by the faithful cooperation of the two together. . . . This is the theme, relating to a small and despised part of the human race and a small and desolate part of the earth, yet world-wide in its significance, that lies hidden in the name of Zion.[15]

Perhaps another reason why the characterization of Zionism as a strictly secular phenomenon is inadequate is that Jewish tradition does not make the same distinction between "secular" and "religious" that has been common in Christian thought. According to Jewish belief, God has always revealed himself through the ordinary events of history, and the impulse to reclaim and redeem the land, even through the efforts of self-professed secularists, is very much in keeping with the Jewish vision of man as God's partner in creation.

The hope of restoring a Jewish national homeland in Palestine, when it first arose with Herzl, presented a serious challenge to traditional Christian theology. It was commonly believed that Jews were doomed to perpetual dispersion and wandering for the "crime" they had committed in biblical times. This was the reaction of Cardinal Merry del Val, then the pope's secretary of state, to Theodore Herzl when Herzl sought Vatican support.

The eventual establishment of the Jewish state of Israel and the overwhelming adoption of *Nostra Aetate* by Vatican Council II have invalidated any approach to either the Jewish people or the state of Israel based on theological convictions of permanent dispersion and suffering.

But the record of Christian opposition to a Jewish state based on a theological rationale—like the long record of persecution and slaughter of Jews by Christians throughout the centuries—is one with which Jews tend to be familiar and Christians tend to be ignorant. Our relative inattention to these matters has left many Christians poorly prepared to understand the strong sense of peoplehood among Jews and their powerful concern for Israel. This concern surfaced dramatically at the time of the Arab-Israeli fighting in 1967, when Jews believed Israel was facing a genocidal threat. As Rabbi Jick has written:

The vision of impending destruction taught us how crucial Israel was to us. The searing experience of mortal danger shook us to the roots of our being. In the fear that we might lose each other, we and the Jewry of Israel found each other. In the prospect of Israel's destruction, we discovered Israel's transcendent significance for our spiritual survival. . . . American Jewry . . . has been moved and will never again be quite the same.[16]

If Christian students are to receive an authentic understanding of Jews and Judaism in today's world, that understanding must encompass the Jewish sense of peoplehood and identification with Israel. Certainly, Christians need not accept any particular view of the significance of Israel; in fact, there is a variety of viewpoints among Jews on this question. But in presenting Judaism to Christian students, we should acknowledge that the vast majority of Jews today feel strong emotional and spiritual ties to Israel.

SOME FINAL REFLECTIONS

An emphasis on particularity, on what is unique and distinctive in the historical experience, culture and life-style of a specific group, is becoming more characteristic, not only of religious, but also of racial and ethnic groups. The intensified sense of peoplehood among Jews and the growing self-assertiveness of blacks, American Indians, Spanish-speaking Americans, and other racial and ethnic groups have challenged the "common core" approach to brotherhood, which minimized differences and stressed shared universals. How are Catholic teachers to react to the rising demand for religious, racial and ethnic identity?

Certainly there exists a potential danger in the particularistic emphasis—the danger of polarization and the loss of a sense of common humanity. Christian educators must be alert to this danger and be prepared to counteract it by affirming the ultimate unity of mankind. But the unity of mankind should not be invoked to obliterate the distinctive integrity of the religious and ethnic heritages we have discussed in the previous chapters. I believe that unity cannot be fully achieved until the various groups that form the community of men have come to feel that their particular traditions are exercising a real influence in shaping the culture and values of the larger society of which they are a part.

Some people who have been active in the struggle for brotherhood and intergroup understanding are discouraged at recent events. I am not, although I recognize the difficulty of the task before us. We can no longer delude ourselves about the easy possibilities of creating brotherhood among men or about the universalistic spirit of our own nation. For us to transform our basically northern European Christian nation into a truly multi-ethnic, multi-racial and multi-religious society will require a tremendous commitment and concentration of effort. Christian educators will continue to occupy a pivotal role in the process. There will be failure and disappointments along the way and we must learn to cope with them, but I am personally convinced that we can reach the goal that now stands before us with greater clarity. Hopefully this book has pointed out some of the concrete steps Catholic educators must take if we are to reach our objective.

FOOTNOTES

1. Cf. Frederick Grant, *op. cit.*; Ellis Rivkin, "The Parting of the Ways," *op. cit.*, pp. 140-141.
2. Cf. Markus Barth, "Was Paul an Anti-Semite?" in *Journal of Ecumenical Studies,* Vol. 5, No. 1 (Winter 1968), p. 93.
3. Bruce Vawter, *op. cit.*, p. 485.
4. Michael Zeik, "Anti-Semitism and the Gospel," in *Commonweal,* March 24, 1967, pp. 16-18.
5. Lee Belford, "Oberammergau's Play Dissected," in *The Churchman,* December, 1970, p. 10.
6. Krister Stendahl, "Judaism and Christianity: A Plea for a New Relationship," in *Cross Currents,* Fall 1967, pp. 445-460.
7. *Ibid.*, p. 452.
8. Cf. Editors of *Commentary, The Condition of Jewish Belief,* New York: Macmillan, pp. 96-97.
9. *Ibid.*, p. 264.
10. Robert Gordis, "Re-Judaising Christianity," reprinted from *The Center Magazine* by the Commission on Inter-Faith Activities, Union of American Hebrew Congregations, p. 5.
11. Edward H. Flannery, "A Survey of Catholic-Jewish Relations, 1970," Secretariat for Catholic-Jewish Relations, Seton Hall University, South Orange, N.J. November 17, 1970 (mimeo).
12. Leon Jick, Abraham J. Klausner, and Elieser Livneh, "American Jewry and Israel's Victory: Aftermath and Opportunity—A Symposium," reprinted from *Dimensions,* Winter 1968, by the Union of American Hebrew Congregations, p. 2.
13. Edward H. Flannery, "Foundations of the State of Israel," Secretariat for Catholic-Jewish Relations, Seton Hall University, South Orange, New Jersey (undated, mimeo).

14. *Ibid.*, p. 6.
15. Cf. Martin Buber, *Israel and Palestine: The History of an Idea,* New York: Farrar, Strauss & Young, 1952, pp. xi-xii.
16. Leon Jick, etc., *op. cit.*, p. 3.

RESEARCH METHODOLOGY

The research procedures used in the three Catholic studies were basically sociological in approach and parallel in intent. But since the procedures differed in detail for each study, the various research designs cannot be interchanged. A brief description of the research procedures follows. Those desiring more technical information regarding statistical findings may consult copies of the dissertations at the St. Louis University Library.

RELIGION STUDY

Sister Rose Thering investigated the most widely used religious textbooks in Catholic secondary schools at the time of her study, together with their related supplementary teaching materials where available. Some sixty-five volumes (books and/or manuals) were selected on the basis of the number of dioceses that sanctioned their use. This corpus comprised seven basic series (four books to a series), two church histories, one guidance series, and four supplementary volumes. Confraternity of Christian Doctrine materials were not included. The central doctrines of Roman Catholicism were not subjected to analysis or evaluation. Thus, a statement that another group was in error was not scored in the analysis. If, however, the group in question was described in a prejudicial and negative light (e.g. "evil Protestants"), then it was noted in the scoring.

Rather than "prejudice" or "bias," the researcher chose the basic concepts of *ethnocentrism,* and its opposite, *altruism,* as the criteria of analysis. These concepts were selected because it was felt they had a more easily measurable content than the other terms. The distinguishing elements of these opposing attitudes are:

1. *Ethnocentrism:* Based on a pervasive and rigid ingroup-outgroup distinction; it involves negative imagery and hostile attitudes toward and regarding outgroups; stereotyped positive imagery and submissive attitudes regarding ingroups; and an hierarchical, authoritarian view of group interaction in which ingroups are rightly dominant and outgroups are subordinate.

2. *Altruism:* Devotion and respect for interests of others; identifying with others; accepting differences; critical of one's own group in an objective manner when necessary.

In order to classify the various kinds of references which are made to other groups, Sister Thering developed nine analytical categories, which were intended to cover, as fully as possible, the entire range of statements made about the outside groups. The nine categories were divided into three broad areas: portrait, relationships and general. Each category has a plus (positive) and minus (negative) side. Thus, in scoring references to Protestants, Jews, Negroes, Orientals, etc. which appear in Catholic textbook materials, the researcher asked herself two questions: (1) In what analytical category does it belong? (2) Is the statement positive or negative, does it contain elements of both, or is it neutral? Analytical categories are described as follows.

A. PORTRAIT

Under the first area, "portrait," or description of other peoples, are two analytical categories:

138

1. *Descriptive Characteristics:* In this category, unit references which describe other groups are scored.

Negative: Statements with: negative emotionalized descriptive terms of individuals and/or groups; the assignment of traits of inferiority; the imputation of non-acceptable roles; negative value judgments or negative stereotypy. *Example:* "bloodthirsty Jews," "Temple gang."

Positive: Statements with: wholesome, kindly descriptions of individuals and/or groups, assertions that defend acceptable roles of other groups; positive objective references with a refutation of negative stereotypy; emphasis placed on an individual as an individual, or recognition of merit irrespective of group images. *Example:* "The Jews under the Old Testament had so great a respect for the name of God that no one except the high priest ever spoke it."

2. *Factual Materials:* This category allows for the scoring of intergroup content as positive, negative, or neutral, when such references are purely factual.

B. RELATIONSHIPS

Under the second broad area of analytical categories, "relationships toward other groups," there are the following four categories:

3. *Creeds-Codes-Prestige Figures:* This category deals with creeds, codes and Catholic authorities as they bear upon the field of intergroup relations. The bearing of the Christian and American creeds as reflected in the faith of the communicator, in the persons of authority, and in official pronouncements or teachings is scored in this category.

Negative: Statements, teachings, creeds, which appeal to the communicator's own group against the concern for the problems of tension, prejudice and hatred of other groups, or the attitudes of inequality toward others exhibited by a creed, code, or person in authority. *Example:* "Catholics should avoid all non-Catholics."

Positive: Statements, teachings, figures of authority, which or who illustrate interest in the breaking down of barriers against communication and dialogue; statements of equality as stressed in the Declaration of Independence, or as discussed in the encyclical on the Mystical Body of Christ. *Examples:* Encyclicals on unity; action of the Holy Father, Pope John XXIII, in the removal of the derogatory terms from the official prayers of the Church.

4. *Rejection/Acceptance:* This category deals with the communicator's relationship with other groups.

Negative: References that show or indicate: punitive statements or expressions of hostility toward other groups; rejection of other groups by forbidding interaction (unless justified by principle or held as a value with one's own group). *Example:* "The first glorious mystery teaches us to meditate on the mysteries of faith, to pray for faith . . . and to avoid the dangers to faith coming from bad reading, or associating too much with non-Catholics, who have no faith themselves."

Positive: References which show friendliness and encourage love and helpfulness to one's neighbor; statements which encourage interaction. *Examples:* Description or mention of the Christian social principle: "The Sermon on the Mount teaches us to be kind to everyone"; "Charity demands that we be kind to every man— Jew, Protestant, or Negro."

5. *Blames Others/Criticizes Self:* The category measures the degree to which the communicator is disposed to involve or separate his own group from the responsibility for the misfortune of the other groups or for existing tensions relative to intergroup relations. This is measured by the presence or absence of self-criticism in the intergroup area as well as by direct statements of responsibility. Self-criticism *not* related to intergroup content is non-scorable.

Negative: References blaming others for existing tensions and problems. *Example:* "Regarding the curse on the Jews: 'They brought it upon themselves.' "

Positive: References acknowledging failure and guilt of one's own group toward other groups. *Examples:* "Abuses prior to the period of the Reformation needed correction"; mention of guilt and involvement of the Catholic group at the time of the Inquisition.

6. *Deplores Differences/Accepts Similarities:* This category seeks to determine whether the intergroup content shows other groups mentioned as related and similar to the Catholics or the ingroups as unrelated and different.

Negative: Statements which deplore differences; which reject contributions of others; which deny historical rootage; which fail to recognize the advantages coming from various contributing groups. *Example:* Negative reports concerning differences.

Positive: References which appreciate differences; which are receptive of contributions of other peoples; which acknowledge historical rootage; which recognize the advantages coming from the various contributing groups.

C. GENERAL

The last main division of the nine analytical categories is the "general" area. In this section are the last three categories, defined as follows:

7. *Distortion/Correction:* This category seeks to measure the amount of distortion or correction of statements and references in the treatment of other groups: religious, racial and ethnic.

Negative: References relevant to intergroup content which conflict with true historical fact; generalizations and unwarranted conjectures. *Example:* Generalizations regarding the entire group stemming from the wrong-doing of one member, or quoting from unauthoritative sources: "All references to Jesus in the Talmud are filled with hate and resentment."

Positive: Statements correcting former distorted interpretations and faulty teachings, or suggesting that these corrections be made. *Examples:* Correction now in the texts regarding the interpretation of the former faulty discussions on the so-called

141

"curse on the Jews."

8. *Failure To Analyze/Analysis of Prejudice:* This category attempts to understand prejudice in its fundamental manifestations. Focus is upon prejudice itself, upon understanding it and analyzing its mechanism, its function and etiology. Statements which are scored in this category constitute an indirect report of self-criticism in the intergroup area.

Negative: The characteristic response is silence, that is, disregard of this area, not measured except by lack of scores on the positive side.

Positive: In this category are scored definitions of prejudice; discussions of the psychological principles of good intergroup relations; discussions of the harm done to the development of a realistic self-concept by the harboring of prejudices.

9. *Activities:* This category is scored whenever activities, questions, and discussions which are relevant to intergroup matters are such that either positive or negative group attitudes are elicited.

Negative: "How did the Jews blackmail Pilate?"

Positive: "Name the Jewish holidays. What do Catholics owe the Jewish people?"

Through statistical procedures, the researcher calculated the extent of preoccupation and the extent of imbalance regarding a variety of other religious, racial and ethnic groups.

The preoccupation figure expresses the ratio of units which contain intergroup content to the total number of units analyzed. Mathematically expressed:

$$Cpr = \frac{r}{t}$$

where *r* is the relevant content and *t* is the total content.

The imbalance figure, expressed numerically, is a complex relation between positive, negative and neutral units; it reflects the degree of preponderence of positive or negative imbalance.

The formula used by the researcher to determine the imbalance figure for the separate analytical categories was:

For positive imbalance, where p is greater than n,

$$Cpi = \frac{p^2 - pn}{rt}$$

For negative imbalance, where n is greater than p,

$$Cni = \frac{pn - n2}{rt}$$

where r is the relevant content and t is the total content.

All the units scored in a single category regardless of direction are relevant content. Total content indicates the total number of units (lessons) containing references to the particular group category being measured.

In addition, the researcher calculated two kinds of general imbalance scores: one, to indicate the general orientation of an individual textbook, or series of textbooks, or publisher for a particular outside group; the second, to determine the direction for combined intergroup areas—for example, all non-Catholic religious groups, racial and ethnic groups, etc.

The formula for the general score of imbalance is:

$$Cgs = \frac{n - p}{r,} \qquad \text{where } n \text{ is greater than } p;$$

$$Cgs = \frac{p - n}{r,} \qquad \text{where } p \text{ is greater than } n,$$

where

n = negative scores;
p = positive scores;
r = relevant content.

For her analysis Sister Rita Mudd collected data from 107 publications (textbooks, workbooks, manuals, and courses of study) then in use in social studies courses in Catholic high schools and grade schools. The subject areas in the grade schools included geography, history, and civics; on the high school level the areas were advanced or economic geography, history, world problems, civics and sociology. Sr. Mudd set up nine "group" categories to classify intergroup references.

Group I was the Protestant group. Here were placed statements relating to the Reformation, to all Protestant denominations, and to individual Protestant leaders. Also included were any references to the history of the various Protestant bodies and to their ritual, symbols, and teachings.

Group II was concerned with the Jewish people. Scored under this heading were all statements pertaining to the religious and ethnic aspects of Judaism. This category took note of all the existing divisions within Judaism in judging any references to biblical or post-biblical Jewry, to its history, religious beliefs, institutions and culture.

Group III comprised the general non-Catholic group. This was a grouping of references to any of the great world religions outside of Judaism and Christianity, such as Islam, Hinduism, Buddhism, Confucianism, Taoism and Shintoism.

Group IV dealt with references to Negroes. It embraced both black Africans and black Americans.

Group V was reserved for American Indians. This category provided for the scoring of references to Indians in the Western hemisphere, their culture and contributions, their past history and present social status.

Group VI was titled the Latin American group. Peoples included in this category were those living south of the Rio Grande and those who reside in the West Indies. Statements treating of inter-American relations were also scored in this category.

Group VII was the Oriental group. It embraced the peoples of the Far East as well as those generally considered part of the

Mongoloid stock. References to the ancient and highly developed civilizations of these people, their contributions and customs, as well as their present-day cultures and government, were evaluated here.

Group VIII, the International group, covered references to the various organizations created to achieve international friendship and cooperation (e.g. League of Nations, World Court, United Nations, etc.).

Group IX was called the General group. Included here were those references to the oneness of the human race or about man in general. Statements referring to the fatherhood of God, the brotherhood of man, and the body of Christ were also placed under this heading.

The quantitative content with respect to the above groups could be measured and reported in a relatively objective fashion. The qualitative analysis of the material presented a much more difficult challenge to Sister Mudd. The crucial problem was how to simplify the results. The categories finally devised by Sister Mudd to describe the direction of the content were defined as possible on the basis of manifest content (rather than implication) and judged by the use of the concepts of *prejudice* and *anti-prejudice.* Sister Mudd relied on the definition of prejudice contained in the principles of the United Nations Commission on Human Rights as a basic criterion:

. . . a way of feeling, a bias or disposition consisting of a commonly shared attitude of hostility, contempt, or mistrust, or devaluation of the members of a particular social or ethnic group because they happen to belong to that group.[1]

This definition presents prejudice as a false and unjust attitude directed *against* members of a particular social or ethnic group. Bias, which is prejudice *toward* members of a particular social or ethnic group, can prove just as destructive of good human relations as prejudice. Biased, unrealistic presentations of Catholicism were therefore scored negatively in Sister Mudd's evaluation.

Anti-prejudice was understood in the social studies analysis as the opposite directional attitude: an attitude of friendliness, acceptance, appreciation, and trust of the members of a particular social or ethnic group because they are part of mankind. Social love or altruism, understood as regard for and devotion to the interests of other people as a group or as individuals would be characteristic of this positive, anti-prejudicial mentality.

The degree of prejudice/anti-prejudice in the instructional materials was determined by the nature of emotional or factual descriptions, by favorable or distorted presentations, by statements advocating acceptance or rejection of individuals or groups, by references which blamed others or were open to self-criticism and by activities and questions that elicited or encouraged favorable or unfavorable attitudes in students toward individuals or groups.

In order to make the criteria for prejudice operative Sister Mudd devised five analytical categories. Prejudice was indicated by a negative score in the appropriate category; a clear attempt to attain or encourage understanding or appreciation of others received a positive score. Statements free from prejudice and not aimed directly at better understanding or appreciation were scored neutral.

The first three categories were primarily concerned with the portrait of individuals and groups in the social studies materials. Within these categories were placed stereotyped statements, statements highlighting the achievements and contributions of particular groups to American and world society, and discussions of roles played by Catholics and outgroups in social tensions.

Negative

"They had the cruel ways that always go with pagan beliefs."

"They [the Jews] are the world's saddest people because they turned away from Jesus."

"Islam has been a source of dissension among the peoples of the world."

"When the Jews refused to accept Jesus he let their enemies overcome them."

Positive

"Afterward they [Japanese] were allowed to settle outside the relocation centers, and since the end of the war, with the realization that not one American of Japanese ancestry was found to be a traitor to the country, many citizens have done what they could to repair the injustice done to them."

"The statement is made that Jews control American industry. The magazine *Fortune* in an impartial survey made some years ago showed that this is not true."

"It was impossible for these natives to stop the advance of the Europeans, and the merciless way in which, until recently, the Indians were enslaved, massacred, driven from their hunting grounds and cheated by the government is a chapter of dishonor."

The fourth category contrasted statements marred by "rejection and inequality" with those which called for "acceptance and equality." Rejection statements were those which expressed hostility or unfriendliness towards individuals or a group. The emphasis here was on group *relationships* rather than portraits of outgroups. The fifth category in the directional area dealt with activities and questions mentioned in the materials, judging these as positive or negative in tone.

Positive

"Sociologists regard notions of race superiority as fundamentally unscientific; Christians regard them as un-Christian in their fundamental sense; and among citizens of the United States they are un-American."

Negative

"How did the Protestant revolt harm Western Europe?"

147

To express the results of her analysis of the social studies textbooks Sister Mudd made use of the coefficient of preoccupation, the coefficient of imbalance, and the general score of imbalance. The latter two of these research tools were employed in exactly the same fashion as in the religion study.

Sister Mudd relied on three different forms of the coefficient of preoccupation in her analysis: (1) total coefficient of preoccupation (a ratio which shows the visibility of all the intergroup content—positive, negative, and neutral—concerning the nine groups of the study as a percentage of the total content); (2) directional coefficient of preoccupation (a ratio which shows the extent of all the directional content—positive and negative—concerning the nine groups of the study as a percentage of the total content); (3) specific group coefficient of preoccupation (a ratio which shows the visibility of a specific group as a percentage of the total group content).

The specific terms of the formulas are explained by Sister Mudd as follows:

1. Total group content includes positive, negative, and neutral references to the nine groups tabulated in the study.

2. Total content includes entire content of publication or publications.

3. Total directional content includes all positive and negative content concerning the nine groups tabulated in the study.

4. Specific group content includes all positive, negative, and neutral references to a specific group.

5. Total group content includes positive, negative, and neutral references to the nine groups tabulated in the study.

LITERATURE TEXTS

Sister Mary Gleason investigated the content of four sets of English literature textbooks and related teaching materials most widely used in Catholic secondary schools at the time the study took place. Her analysis concentrated on the *speaking* characters on the assumption that speaking characters influence a reader's attitude to a greater degree than characters who are merely described by others. Just as people in real life reveal themselves by speaking, so too do people in fiction.[2]

148

Sister Gleason analyzed some 3,154 characters in her study. Her basis criterion for evaluation was the definition of the term prejudice given by the psychologist Gordon Allport:

An avertive or hostile attitude toward a person who belongs to a group, simply because he belongs to the group, and is therefore presumed to have objectionable qualities ascribed to the group.[3]

Prejudice thus has two faces, both of which are *a priori* fixations not rooted in real knowledge or experience. Negatively, prejudice means looking unfavorably at others without sufficient warrant; positively it involves a favorable attitude that lacks a firm basis. Under the category of prejudice as applied in the literature study came stereotyped expressions, generalizations, and instances of name-calling. The use of dialect in the literature materials was also examined to see if in some instances it might open the way for group tension and the possibility of prejudicial thinking. For the purpose of tabulation the speaking characters were classified according to groups: racial, socio-economic, religious, community background and ethnic origins. In addition, each character was evaluated according to role (major/minor), educational status, character traits (prudent/imprudent, honest/dishonest, respectable/unrespectable, desirable/undesirable), and method of characterization.

In actual fact, few of the speaking characters were able to be evaluated according to all of the above categories. Sister Gleason was forced to devise an *undetermined* category which included all the characters whose backgrounds could not be identified because of insufficient evidence.

To ensure greater objectivity in her findings Sister Gleason submitted her research design and implementation of that design in the course of the research to a panel of eight people for criticism. This panel represented two racial groups, three religious groups and varied ethnic and community backgrounds.

The panel operated in the following manner. The members were given a two-week period in which to study and classify the characters according to a coding key drawn up by Sister Mudd. Joint discussions followed which revealed some differences in the interpretation of definitions by panelists. These differences were discussed until agreement could be reached. As a result of this panel procedure, the definitions were expanded and the coding system altered.

After the character analysis was completed and the 3,154 characters coded, the results were mechanically computed in order to obtain the number and percentages of individuals in each of the categories. This process was completed and tabulated book by book and set by set.

When this information had been recorded, the process of cross-tabulation began. The purpose of this procedure was to give a clearer picture percentage-wise of the relationships existing between the characters of various racial, socio-economic status, religious, community background, and ethnic groupings and their role in the selection, educational status, and the character traits of prudence, honesty, respectability and desirability.

One question must be raised in trying to assess the findings of the literature study. Do students really grasp a cumulative picture of a group or form general attitudes toward that group as a result of their encounter with individual members of the group in the context of various literary selections? It is conceivable that the very nature of literature, in which each literary document possesses a unity of its own, may militate against such group identification. Sister Gleason believes that there exists sufficient evidence to warrant the assumption that students do build a cumulative orientation toward groups through meeting individual characters from that group. It is an assumption, however, and she accepts the necessity for further testing its validity.

FOOTNOTES

1. Cf. Marie Jahoda, Morton Deutsch, and Stewart Cook, *Research Methods in Social Relations,* New York: Dryden, p. 365.
2. Cf. Manuel Komroff, *How To Write a Novel,* New York: Simon and Schuster, p. 38.
3. *The Nature of Prejudice,* Boston: Beacon Press, p. 7.

INDEX

T 46497

MEPKIN ABBEY
1098 Mepkin Abbey Road
Moncks Corner, S.C. 29461